Stock Market Miracles

Other Books by Wade B. Cook:

Wall Street Money Machine

Real Estate Money Machine

Blueprints For Success (1997)

Brilliant Deductions (1997)

Real Estate For Real People

How To Pick Up Foreclosures

101 Ways To Buy Real Estate Without Cash

555 Clean Jokes

<u>Also in Manual/Seminar Format:</u>

The Wall Street Workshop Video/Home Study Course

The Next STEP Video/Home Study Course

The Incorporation Handbook

Zero To Zillions

Financial Fortress

Real Estate Cash Flow System

Retirement Prosperity

Stock Market Miracles

Wade B. Cook

The Lighthouse Publishing Group,
an imprint of
Wade Cook Seminars, a subsidiary of
Profit Financial Corporation,
a publicly traded company.
Ticker symbol PFNL
Seattle, Washington

Distributed to the trade by
Midpoint Trade Books, Inc.
(212) 727-0190

Manufactured in the
United States of America

The Lighthouse Publishing Group
Copyright © 1997 by Wade B. Cook. All rights reserved.
Printed in the United States of America.   1st Edition

Library of Congress Catalog-in-Publication Data

Cook, Wade B.
Stock Market Miracles
ISBN (cloth) 0-910019-71-1
Parts of this book have been released in slightly different versions as Special
Reports for use in conjunction with teaching done by Wade Cook himself or
various staff members.
Includes bibliographical references and index.
1. Stock options I. Title.
HG6042.C66   1996
332.63'228--dc20
95–47134

"This publication is designed to provide accurate and authoritative
information in regard to the subject matter covered. It is sold with the
understanding that the publisher is not engaged in rendering legal,
accounting, or other professional service. If legal or expert assistance is
required, the services of a competent professional person should be
sought."
From a declaration of principles jointly adopted by a committee of the
American Bar Association and committee of the Publishers Association.

The Lighthouse Publishing Group
a subsidiary of Profit Financial Corporation
14675 Interurban Avenue South
Seattle, WA 98168

10 9 8 7 6 5 4 3 2 1

To Helene and Carl Cook,
My Mom and Dad

They raised me to appreciate life,
to live with passion,
to live by the rules,
and to help others.

CONTENTS

CHAPTER OUTLINES

(a) supply and demand

(b) time remaining before expiration date

(c) market sentiments

(d) Good Till Cancelled (GTC) option

   2. Cash flow

   a) options cost less than stocks to purchase

   b) a slight movement in the stock price means a significant movement in the option price

   c) options require only one day to clear the bank

   3. There is no obligation to buy the actual stock or the options

B. Buy On Dips

C. Rolling Options

D. Straddles

   1. Writing a call and a put option

   a) on the same stock

   b) for the same price

   c) with the same expiration date

   2. Potential risks

   a) if the stock price drops, you may be forced to buy the put option you sold

   b) if the stock price increases, you may be forced to buy the actual stock at the new price and sell it at the call price

E. Hedge a Stock

   1. A method that limits your downside by purchasing the actual stock and selling options on that stock

F. Combo

Preface

When I finished my last book, *Wall Street Money Machine,* I thought I had written everything I could write about my strategies for investing in the stock market. Then several things happened.

The first was a dramatic increase in our seminar business. This drove me to create, develop, try, and perfect new methods for portfolio cash flow enhancement, big words for getting more income out of investments and using the excess cash flow to buy really good "keeper" stocks.

The second was, and I hope will continue to be, my thirst for knowledge—especially knowledge and wisdom which work in the marketplace. Fine tuning and getting bigger, better, and quicker returns, using stocks, and purchasing variations to really generate a lot of income are major motivating factors in my life.

This second point leads to my third and final point. I want to be one of the very best educators in America. I do deals and learn so I can teach. I'm more into how a certain formula can be duplicated and then shared with others than into money for money's sake. I have a lot of money, and while that's nice, my real passion is helping others improve their lives.

This passion has me constantly searching, questioning, and visiting with others to figure out their real needs. I wrote this book to address those problems and concerns.

Right now, I'm sitting in an airport. I do a lot of that as I travel the width and breadth of this country teaching. The balance of this book has been written and it's almost time to go to press. It's high time I wrote the preface so it will not hold up the process!

Why, you might ask, am I writing the preface last? Shouldn't it be done first to give direction to the book's plot? Maybe for some authors, but not for me. Not this time.

You see, I believe in serendipity. If you've read my first book on cash flowing stocks (**Wall Street Money Machine**), then you know how my system works. I have some ideas, then I try and test them until I find one which works - repetitiously. I guide my efforts to find new ways. Serendipity, to me, means a happy or joyous discovery on the way to something else. A dictionary defines it as such: "The faculty of making fortunate discoveries by accident."

As I tried new ways and perfected old ones, I wrote. Month after month I wrote and here's the book—a collection of new formulas, variations on old ones, and the rationalizations and reasonings behind them. This turned out to be the book I wish I had written first.

Why the weird title? After all, there are not really miracles in the stock market. Perhaps miracles happen on 34th Street, but not on Wall Street. However, the returns these strategies create seem like miracles.

A miracle is a phenomenon which defies explanation. We usually think of miracles in a spiritual way, so let me go there and then segue my way back and show how this title came to be.

The Bible is the basis for the following: God intervenes in the lives of mortals. Sometimes what happens can't be explained. There is no rational explanation. I know there are pure miracles, but sometimes I wonder if God does not use ordinary things like people, events, nature, et cetera to bring about good things. A grocery sack of food left on someone's doorstep could be a miracle and an answer to someone's prayer. A wise teacher, a passage of scripture and a good friend could all provide many mini-miracles.

I have been able to obtain fantastic returns on so many stock market plays: 260,000% annualized one hour returns; 10,680% annualized in two days and so many more. (Note: See Appendix One. It's a listing of the last 50 actual trades, winners and losers all included. I made these trades before I went on a recent TV interview. There are forty-six winners and four small losers where $20,000 becomes over $100,000 in a short time—$83,000 net profit.)

To some, these seem to defy logic, or at least they defy explanation. Not to me. They make sense. I do them every day and so will you. These trades are sort of like a magic trick. At first it seems "stupendous"—other worldly. But as you learn the trick you say "it's a piece of cake."

They are, however, miracles to some people because of what they are able to do in their own lives. I love attending our Wall Street Workshops. Some people shake my hand so hard it takes a while to recover. People who needed $30,000 in four weeks to adopt three Cambodian babies had it four weeks after the class; a man who can spend (and has done so for over a year) $2,000 a month to help his mother, who is seventy-eight years old, retire better; another man with $30,000 who made $700,000 in about five months. Countless hundreds of people have retired on $7,000 to $15,000 per month, in less than six months, starting with usually around $5,000. The changes are real. They are not real miracles, but they have the same effect and the same impact.

If the returns you receive from implementing the following strategies seem to defy gravity, then great for you. You keep the profits. I get the satisfaction of knowing you're doing well.

I want to change the way you think. Read what was in the January 1st issue of *Forbes* Magazine 60 years ago: "Optimism is a tonic. Pessimism is poison. Admittedly, every business man must be realistic. He must gather facts, analyze them candidly, and strive to draw logical conclusions, whether favorable or unfavorable. Granting this, the incontestable truth is that America has been built up by optimists, not by pessimists." I am sure my dedication to excel and my passion for sharing will have us meet one day. I am a millionaire-maker. Our meeting will probably be at one of my training sessions. I wish you well as you stun and amaze those around you with these simple, yet effective, cash-flow strategies. I live my life by and wholeheartedly agree with Albert Einstein's statement: "Many times a day I realize how much my own life is built upon the labors of my fellowmen, and how earnestly I must exert myself in order to give in return as much as I have received."

ACKNOWLEDGMENTS

This book is not the product of studies or schoolroom research, but of live, active, try-it-till-it-works, in-the-trenches formulas and techniques. Students in the past have appreciated strategies that really work—simple, yet powerful, in that they produce results. I would like to acknowledge and give a heartfelt thanks to those on my staff whose dedication it is to help others. Lisa Michaels, Pete O'Brien, and Laura Howell on my research/ trading and Wealth Information Network (W.I.N.) have played an important role. My Wall Street Workshop instructors and technicians get Kudos for their everyday work. To name a few; Paul Cook, Steve Wirrick, Bob Eldridge, Keven Hart, David Elliott, Tim Semingson, Joel Black, Eric Glenn, and Jay Harris. My gratefulness also extends to my students who wrote, faxed, and E-mailed me deals and strategies they use. Cheryle Hamilton, my editor at Lighthouse Publishing has rendered tireless service to bring these manuscripts to fruition. The publishing and graphics department who carefully proof and create these books; Mark Engelbrecht, Alison Curtis, Angela Wilson, and Connie Suehiro also deserve many thanks as well as the production staff, thanks. To my department heads at Wade Cook Seminars who filled and do such a great job as I take time out to write and travel: Christopher

Cardé, Clayton Sherwood, Kim Brydson, David Hebert, Shane Norris, Eric Rodriguez, Eric Marler, Caesar Regoso, and so many others. My wife, Laura, and daughter, Leslie, also try these ideas and show me better ways to do things.

TO ALL WHO HAVE BEEN A PART, THANKS!

WHAT PARTICIPANTS SAY ABOUT THE WALL STREET WORKSHOP:

"As an adult educator with a graduate degree in education as well as an M.B.A., I have found the three days of the Wall Street Workshop fast paced with information I have not found elsewhere—a real mind trip. 15 years as a self-employed businessman and in three days I multiplied my business knowledge many fold. Thanks."
—Stefan G.

"You have shown me how to generate my retirement income. In the last half of this year, I generated $70,000."
—Jim N.

"When Wade said 'This course can cost you $100,000 if you don't go,' he was right. I bought a whole bunch of Fannie Mae calls on a Friday at $1/4$ and sold them the next Monday at $3/4$. That's 200% in just a few days. Thanks Wade."
—Greg G.

"In the past year, my IRA account increased by 84%, my wife's by 132%. My Nevada corporation earned $30,000 in its first year in business, not to mention what it saved in state income taxes. Obviously, I'm sold."
—Ken W.

"I've learned many ways to help my portfolio in this seminar. I've done many covered calls and in one month made $15,000 to $16,000. Wade helped change my way of investing."
—Clifton F.

"This has been an exciting two weeks for me and my family. It has been two weeks since I attended that Wall Street Workshop. I can't begin to tell you the amount of electricity and confidence that is generated around my home recently. Before the workshop, I considered myself an average stock trader, at times performing fairly well, but otherwise just treading water. I have never had any formal training in the stock market, and after listening to most others (including brokers), I considered the option market strictly a "voodoo curse" to be wary of.

In your workshop, the second day of class I made my first two rolling options purchases. To my pleasant surprise, I was able to sell both options the following morning for a profit large enough to cover the complete cost of the workshop.

At home, after the excitement of the workshop, I began buying options as we were taught in class. So far I have used only one investment strategy (buying options on rolling stocks) and have completed 10 buys and sells. In the last 15 days I have been able to obtain a clear net profit of $23,252.35, after commissions. Yes, that's right! 74.4% in 15 days! I'm still pinching myself to see if I'm awake."
—Michael K.

"Wall Street Workshop flash: We made $3,100 in about 6 hours with the information taught in this workshop. Mike took this workshop in mid-January and made $35,000 in two months using rolling stocks and covered calls. The class was fabulous, the instructors were

terrific, and we're coming out for the advanced workshop to learn even more. Thanks a lot."
—Mike and Pat O.

"I love this stuff. I made a 27% profit on my money in less than 5 weeks! I can't wait till tomorrow to do it again."
—Robert G.

"I finally understand options! I gained enough courage [at the seminar] to write some covered calls for a total profit of 78%."
—J.J.

"I fully understand the benefits of covered calls, stock splits, rolling stocks, and options. It has been beneficial for me to be here. When Wade was speaking he was moving at a pace I could understand and implement."
—Donald S.

"This has been a very intense, but very informative workshop. I took advantage of this learning experience to get my feet wet in the securities market with a small investment and made $600. This has definitely been worthwhile."
—Stanley N.

"I heard about this seminar from my husband—he bought the tape series and made me listen to them. They were great! This seminar helped us to see that dealing with the stock market is something that we can do—as long as we do the research first."
—Dana T.

"I knew nothing, nada, zilch about stocks when I met Wade; now, after the Wall Street Workshop, I understand what to look for a lot better. The strategies & formulas will be very helpful for creating cash flow, which is why I came, and I thank you for teaching me. I *will not give up (or quit bugging you guys) until I master them, especially rolling stocks & options.*

I delivered pizzas all through college, and I quickly figured out that no matter what I did, I was averaging $1/run; therefore, like Wade, I was doubling & tripling the amount everyone else was making waiting around on the 'big' tips. I really, really click with Wade's thinking—I love the meter drop mentality. I've been singing it all along; I just didn't know what to call it or where to use it. Obviously, that philosophy will pay much larger dividends (pun intended) in stocks than pizza delivery. Thanks Wade & Team!"
—Jackie L.

"My understanding of the stock market rose from 1 $^1/_8$ to 102 $^1/_4$."
—Joe O.

"This seminar gave me an understanding of stocks & options that I could not have gotten elsewhere. The days of my losing money on deals I don't know or completely understand are over! Now I know how to make excellent returns & minimize my risk! I am excited and looking forward to managing my portfolio correctly—for the first time!"
—Scott S.

"My wife and I can now see a future where we are working together from home and being very successful. I will be doing this on a full time basis and our goal is to have my wife out of work in 3-5 years. We earned $2,500 in our 1st two days of trading and we never traded in the stock market before. The experience has given us the opportunity to make a fortune, help our family, and live the kind of life we always dreamed of. Our dreams will become a reality thanks to Wade and his great staff, and we are only 32 and 31 years old!"
—Leo K.

The following are participant comments on The Next STEP Wall Street Workshop seminar.

"[The Next STEP] added to the strategies presented in the WSWS. Gaps and Split strategies added new greatness to the trading of my stocks. It opened my eyes to playing the market on the upward and downward trends in the market. I better understand the put strategies and the straddle plays."
—Jay R.

"I was worrying if the seminar would be worth the price. After 30 minutes of the first day, I knew I had already received more value than the price. The value increased by the minute thereafter. Thank you for a great seminar."
—Robert P.

"[I attended my] first WSWS in Houston, September 22-23. I started with $50,000 and my account is now at $177,000. Not "perfect," but I consider myself still on the learning curve. That is why I attended The Next STEP WSWS. I intend to place another $250,000 into play in the next two months, I started my first corporation, living trust, and limited partnerships two weeks ago. Six other people have attended the WSWS at my urging and are making bucks already. All of this in six months!
—Lance B.

"I invested $5,000 in rolling USRX, in two days I made $4750. In one day [with SWK] I made $1,875 and I turned a covered call with ASFT and made $3,500 in two days (for a total net profit of $9,625). The only thing I can say is Thank you!"
—Jim C.

Call 1-800-872-7411 for more information about these courses.

1

BUILDING A GREAT PORTFOLIO

When my first book on stock market investing hit the street, I was overwhelmed by the incredible favorable response. I received countless letters and E-mail messages. These were no ordinary "thank you's," as most had included specific trades they had made, records of deals, and cash-flow profits to be proud of. *"I've made $43,000 in one month," "$19,000 in three days," "We just adopted kids with the $30,000 we made this month."* Too many wonderful stories to mention here. See the testimonials at the beginning of the book for a sampling of the many exciting stories we hear.

But there have been the critics also. Don't misunderstand. I've not been criticized by anyone who actually read the book, and surely not by anyone who has followed the formulas and done the trades. Actually, the only real criticism has come from comments made on the jacket; like *"outrageous returns,"* or *"double your money every 2¹/₂ to 4 months."*

USING OPTIONS TO BUILD A PORTFOLIO

So to answer this light and superfluous charge, I dedicate this chapter to building a strong portfolio for the long term.

I won't turn on my cash flow formulas. In fact, I'll use them to build a portfolio to be proud of — an "investment club" style portfolio, but I'll do so my way; defining the methods and even the terms, such as "long term."

I am no different than most prudent investors or pension and mutual fund managers. I want to look at my portfolio and see huge, brand-name stocks like AT&T, Boeing, Wrigleys, McDonalds, Nordstrom, Sears, General Electric, Pfizer, Marriott, et cetera. I want to own stock in companies I can eat in, shop at, dial up, and sleep in! I like quality. I repeat, I like great companies with excellent growth, trademarks, earnings, market niche, and sheer strength of size. I want millions of dollars of them and I don't want to have to work a 9 to 5 job to get them. Boy, that's a conundrum. It's almost impossible to work a typical American job, with average income and accumulate millions. Yes, in 40 to 50 years maybe, but who wants to wait that long? That's the rub—accomplishing the task of having millions, without having to work for millions. So, it is not my <u>goal</u> or objective which differs from the "conventional wisdom" reeking from virtually every financial planner/stockbroker—the so-called experts — but the <u>method</u> of getting there. This is where we part ways.

You see, my method is simple. I want to use a small amount of money—risk capital if you will, to generate cash flow which will exponentially generate more income. I've never advocated that a person put his portfolio at risk with aggressive plays. In fact I've repeatedly and strongly advised against it.

To prove this point, and so there is no misunderstanding, I'll repeat it here. Use a small amount of money—say $2,000 to $10,000—to build a cash flow machine. Keep the balance of your money in high grade stocks, bonds, mutual funds, and even in real estate and other businesses outside the traditional stock market investments. The stock market is simply too risky for me.

Will Rogers said it best: "I'm worried about the return *of* my money, not just the return *on* it."

Let's deal with the $2,000 to $10,000 figures. That may seem high to participants of the "meet the 2nd Tuesday of each month, invest $50 a month and sit around for hours discussing one or two stocks, and hope for the best" clubs so prevalent today. Let's break everyone into categories: Those with *under $100,000* to invest, and those with *over $100,000* to invest. Everyone reading this falls into one of these two categories. That's simple, but the next part is not so simple. If you only have $2,000 or so to get started, then I'll make an assumption — your family is young. If you're older, (say older than 40) and you can barely scrape together $2,000, then you probably need a different book than this one—perhaps a motivational book, or one on vitamin pills. Whatever, young or old, if that's it, then find the most outrageous, crazy, wild, risky plan you can find and go for the gusto. What do you have to lose? Surely you can get back (earn, etc.) $2,000 to $5,000. In Arizona, they teach you that if you have water (bottle, canteen, etc.) and you get stranded in the desert — drink it all—now! Apparently our bodies store and ration liquids better than our minds.

If you have $100,000, then take $95,000 and buy safe, secure, blue chip, "hold for the long term" stocks. Be extra safe. Now take $2,000 to $5,000 and go to town. Treat the stock market like a business. Be aggressive.

Read the following letter and see what I mean. The last time I talked to this man, his $20,000 was over $267,000 and that's three to four months after attending my Wall Street Workshop. He's on target to make over $1,000,000 in one year, from his $20,000.

Dear Mr. Cook,

Enclosed please find a copy of my extended re-sume and a video copy of my film product reel. No, I'm not looking for employment, I've included it so that you can see that my occupation is not one conducive to "playing the stock market." I'm a movie maker. I write, direct, and produce features for theatre and television.

Pretty far removed from the market, wouldn't you say? So, why am I sending it? For one reason . . . I'm now six weeks or so past one of your Houston Wall Street Workshops and the results have been interesting (an understatement)!

As a filmmaker, I move from project to project. I've just completed a two-hour television special en-titled, **America, A Call To Greatness** *with Charlton Heston, Mickey Rooney, Deborah Winters, and Peter Graves. Next week, I'll be directing several episodes of a new fall series for ABC. In between, I do nothing. It's these periods of inactivity that annoy me. It's not that I have to be constantly active, but it helps. In my industry, these periods are referred to as "being between pictures." Translated, it means unemployed— "waiting." I've been in the industry for some years and I always have work . . . and I always have inactivity. Having heard of your workshop, I thought perhaps it might provide me something to do during these periods. Although I've been in the market from time to time, one of your sales people convinced me* *that I didn't have to know anything about the market to attend . . . and to benefit. Another customer service representative recommended that I come prepared to trade . . . to open a stock account, etc., so I did.*

You will note from my resume that I spent ten years as a university professor and about the same on the "seminar" and "consulting" circuit. I know from experience that only a few out of a seminar ever really benefit . . . not because the seminar isn't good, but because most tend not to apply what they learn. I didn't want to be one of those, so I took the tapes mailed with your "Financial Power Pack" and listened to them . . . and listened to them . . . and listened to them. Even during the class breaks, I continued to replay them, etc. They were helpful in that I had an idea about what would be discussed during class and became familiar with some of the terminology.

I've always enjoyed a "good" seminar and this one was. I must admit I was skeptical, mostly because of the perceived "hype" that went with the "selling." However, the class did deliver on what it promised (a seminar that "works,"what a novel approach).

I opened an account with $5,000. If I made money (which I had reservations about), great. If I lost money then it wouldn't be "great" but it would occupy some of the time before I began directing again. I must admit, I didn't expect what followed.

I began trading on the first day and knew immediately that I'd opened an account with the wrong broker when he began to argue with me about my trade. What I didn't want to do was jump into his company "hot stock of the day." While I knew nothing about the market, I didn't just fall off the banana boat either. Fortunately, there was a broker attending the WSWS that understood what the class was doing and was able to produce buy/sell slips demonstrating that he was actually making the trades being discussed in class. I opened an account with him and the choice has turned out to be a very good one. There was no "training" of the broker required. In fact he was (and has been) very supportive of the "Cook-Concepts." (In fact, he'll be attending the Wealth Academy with me in June.)

I won't bore you with the class trading details but by Friday following Thursday's class end, my $5,000 had grown to nearly $15,900. That got my attention! I added another $15,000 to the account and a little over a month later, my account was nearing $100,000. I added another sum of money and similar results have followed since then.

I wanted to learn each of the strategies taught, so I tried a number of them.

For example:

Sample Option Plays:

Bought Coke (KO) Options at $4.625 and sold after a split at $6.50

Bought Iomega (IOMG) Options at $6 and sold at $10.25

Bought Accustaff (ACST) Options at $3.25 and sold at $4.875

Sample Covered Calls:

QuaterDeck (QDEK) bought stock at $14 and sold options twice

Egghead (EGGS) stock at $12 and sold calls at $1.9375

Network Express (NETK) at $12, sold calls at $.875 and called out at $12.50

IMP Inc. (IMPX) stock at $17.50, sold calls at $.9375

Sample Rolling Stock:

Bought ScoreBoard (BSBL) at $4.125 and sold at $5.636 (dropped & bought again)

Network Express (NETK) at $3.23 and sold at $5

. . . and I could go on with some 23 other trades. I lost on five of them. Of the five, three of the losses were my fault, not the system. And listen, Mr. Cook, if you think driving a taxi doesn't qualify a person to be in the market, try movie directing. This morning I bought 10 contracts of HBOC at $12 and now three hours later I just sold the calls at $13.50. It's only a 12.5% return, but annualized it's 4,562.5%. Not too shabby for a few hours work.

As I said earlier, I'd had a successful career in the consulting and seminar field so I always appreciate a good seminar (most are not). And, as much as I like the Wall Street Workshop, I would have paid the fee just for the last day's entities' seminar. Aside from my market success, I will save enough in taxes from that one day to pay not only for the Wall Street Workshop, but for every other seminar that you offer, the courses you sell, the books, manuals and chapters, W.I.N., etc. And, you will note from your sales records in my account that I've gotten about everything you have (paid for by the WSWS course).

Since the course, I've read your new "hit" in detail, studied the **Zero to Zillions** *home study course, watched and re-watched the WSWS Video Tape Sets, etc. Since the first course was so good, I've signed up for the June* "Wealth Academy" *and will be attending* "The Next S.T.E.P. Wall Street Workshop," *etc. It's going to take a lot more than the 5 star entities to handle my business (I already have six), so I'll also be at the* "Executive Retreat." *The best of all this is that I haven't paid for a dime of it. The earnings have more than covered everything.*

I like your style so much that I've registered for the June "Real Estate Boot Camp" *but this time, I'm bringing my wife. Now talk about someone without a background for real estate . . . my wife, Deborah, is an actress (she had one of the leads in* The Winds of War *and lead in* Kotch *with Walter Mathau, the lead in* Class of '44, *and the lead in* The Outing, *etc.) But, she, like myself, has interests in things outside our field . . . particularly where they are profitable. To keep it in the family, my son will be attending your youth WSWS in August. It's a great idea. I would have liked to have had this background when I was his age.*

The concept of teaching the youth financial concepts when they are young is terrific. If I can help you in any way, please don't hesitate to ask.

Mr. Cook, thanks for being in the "business." The only problem is that now I'm enjoying the market more than the other things that I'm doing . . . a nice problem!

Best Regards,
Dr. Warren C.

OK, let's say he only makes $250,000 on the initial $5,000. Let's say that's you. You're two days of training away from having the skills to do this. If it is you, and you are into safety, remember, you have your $95,000 worth of good, solid investments to make you feel good at night and when you get your portfolio's statements. Hopefully, the dividends and growth of the stocks will give you 10% plus per year. That could be $10,000 (of which only a small portion is cash). You've got the best of both worlds; aggressive cash flow <u>and</u> stability.

ADD TO YOUR POSITIONS

Now, let's move on. Take $100,000 or even $200,000 and buy more blue chips. Take the other $50,000 (or more) and keep it generating cash flow. You see, that's the point I've been making at my seminars and in my writings. Use the formulas for income generation to build up your cash flow, so you can accelerate the purchase of stocks in great companies.

Here is a list of my cash flow strategies:

(1) Rolling stocks

(2) Slams—buying stock on dips

(3) Bottom Fishing

(4) Peaks (short sells or buy puts)

(5) Rolling Options

(6) Writing Covered Calls

(7) Selling Naked Puts

(8) Dividends (I have many Special Reports and taped seminars explaining these)

(9) Stock Splits

(10) Turnarounds and Spin-offs . . .

They are to be used for cash flow. They put the emphasis on selling—getting out. You only purchase them to resell them at a profit. They deal with two-week and one-month 15% to 55% returns. They spin off cash. Real money. "Send it to my house and let's go shopping" type of money!

If you choose, you can use some or all of this cash flow to build a wonderful, safe, "proud to own" retirement portfolio. But one which accumulates quickly because you're able to add to it repeatedly, month after month, with the profits from the smaller cash flow part of your system. Look at the following:

STARTING PORTFOLIO—Start with $2,000 to $10,000

Aggressive Strategies	Building Portfolio
Options	Keep
Covered Calls	aggressive
Rolling Stock	with
Rolling Options	profits

BUILDING PORTFOLIO—$15,000-$30,000

Aggressive Strategies	Building Portfolio
Stay aggressive with $12,000	Move profits from aggressive to buy:
Options	Blue Chips
Covered Calls	DOW Industrials
Rolling Stock	S&P 500
Rolling Options	High Quality Growth

MATURING PORTFOLIO—$30,000 and up

Aggressive Strategies	Building Portfolio
Stay aggressive with $15,000	Move profits from aggressive to buy:
Options	Blue Chips
Covered Calls	DOW Industrials
Rolling Stock	S&P 500
Rolling Options	High Quality Growth
	REITS (Tax Advantages)

SAMPLE AGGRESSIVE STOCKS

INTC

DELL

IOMG

AMTX

COMS

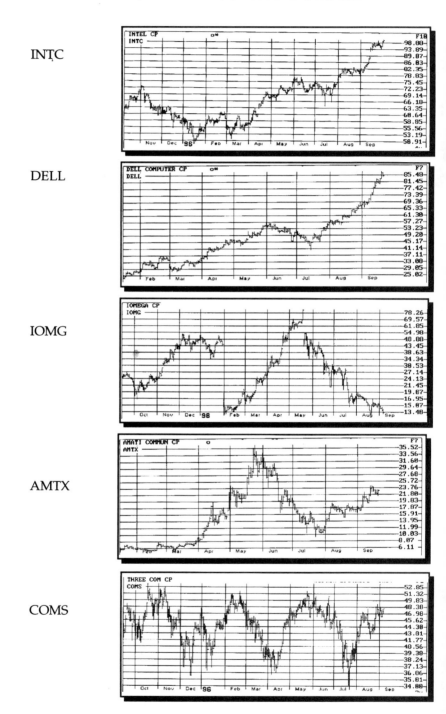

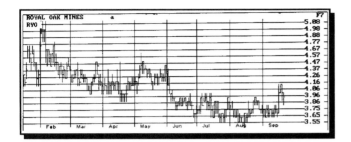

RYO

SAMPLE BUILDER STOCKS

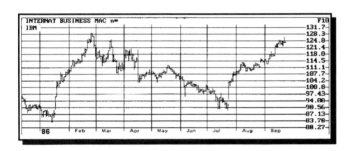

IBM

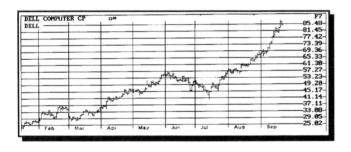

DELL

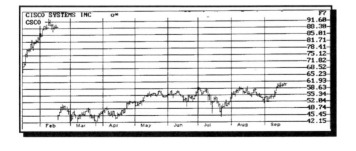

CSCO

MSFT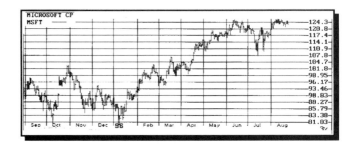

BRU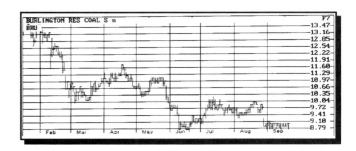

Look at the diagram on the following page. Study it. You'll see at first, and in most cases continually, a strategy to keep up the income but move profits into safer investments.

BUILD A GREAT PORTFOLIO

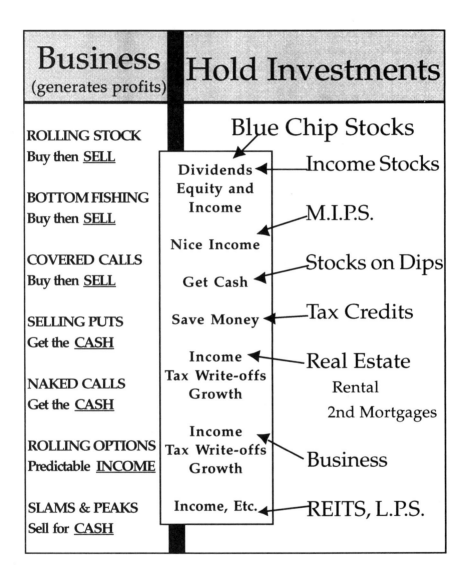

Business (generates profits)	Hold Investments
ROLLING STOCK Buy then <u>SELL</u>	Blue Chip Stocks
	Dividends ← Income Stocks
BOTTOM FISHING Buy then <u>SELL</u>	Equity and Income
	← M.I.P.S.
COVERED CALLS Buy then <u>SELL</u>	Nice Income
	Get Cash ← Stocks on Dips
SELLING PUTS Get the <u>CASH</u>	Save Money ← Tax Credits
	Income ← Real Estate
NAKED CALLS Get the <u>CASH</u>	Tax Write-offs Growth Rental 2nd Mortgages
	Income
ROLLING OPTIONS Predictable <u>INCOME</u>	Tax Write-offs Growth ← Business
SLAMS & PEAKS Sell for <u>CASH</u>	Income, Etc. ← REITS, L.P.S.

ALL THIS FOR A BETTER LIFE

2

TREAT IT AS A BUSINESS

Can you get rich working for someone else?

Probably not, unless you make excess income and then get that extra income producing great returns.

Can you get rich owning your own business?

Yes, but most businesses fail. Even if the business does not fail, most take up too much of the owner's (manager's) time working on things which do not make him or her rich.

Is the American Dream still alive and well?

It truly is.

One secret of wealth accumulation has been that little extra something put aside and left to compound. Is the time right for you to "get rich?" After all, someone becomes a millionaire every 37 minutes. When is it going to be your turn? What superior knowledge do you have? What risks are you willing to take? What time can you donate to making a great financial life? This chapter is about getting rich—filthy rich if you want, with more income than you can possibly spend. I have thought long and hard about what I could write, what I could do to help you become a "cash flow millionaire." I want you to read every word of this. Do not skip anything. I will build a case for you and show you in many ways that you can build up $12,000 to $35,000 per month cash flow—and do it in the next year. I will show you how to do it without vitamin pills, or any other multilevel concern. I will show you how to do it by first eliminating the risk—or at least making risk so negligible as to make it a non-item.

You will use Bear Market strategies in the midst of a Bull Market, and you can get started with $500 if that is all you have. It is doable. I have made tens of thousands of dollars a day—if you attend a stock market training session we will show you how you can build up this level of income. And you do not have to go through nine years of costly trial and error like I did. You will not have to be at the mercy of unscrupulous and unintelligent stock brokers, as I have been. You can cut to the chase, start making huge returns in days and keep all your profits.

You might be asking yourself, "How can Wade possibly be talking about the stock market? Especially when funds managers claim bragging rights with 12% returns?" Can investing really produce 18% - 42% monthly returns—month in and month out? And what kind of returns are these? I will answer all of those questions, but for now allow me to start with the last question. The kind of returns I am speaking of are actual cash—either hitting your account or mailed to your home or business. It is not growth, not tax savings, but money you can use.

For awhile—at least in the beginning—I suggest you use it for portfolio enhancement, either building more cash flow by doing more of what you did before, or buying some "hold" investments; or applying it to other formulas. Later, with a small amount of money, delve into riskier but incredibly profitable strategies to really make a big "bang" on your bottom line. Regardless of your choice, your return is in cash, not some poor substitute. I have always contended that WE, you and I and all my other students, can make more together than we ever can alone. It is true. I will lead the way. I will try and test new ideas, formulas, strategies, processes—you come along, buy my book, attend my ongoing classes, and then make millions, spending your profits the way you like.

Each person who attends my seminars does so for his own personal reasons. Some are just getting started and need to learn the basics, others are in business or want to be, and need help "growing" their business. Others are making good money but paying a high price in terms of stress, time away from their families, etc. Others have tax problems and a host of others are in various stages and want to learn how to keep and protect what they have as well as pass on what they have "scraped" together throughout their lives. And while they come for various reasons, they all have one thing in common—they know there is a better way. A more excellent way, if you will. What is the saying, "Winners just find a better way to get there?"

Now that I have asked all these questions, who is this person asking these questions? Let me introduce myself briefly. I realize you may not know anything about me or my background, or to what extent it will help you make more money. So I will be brief, but you need to walk in my shoes for a moment. I cannot help you in the present unless you know what got me here, what drives me, what my fears and passions are.

H ISTORY

When I was young, my goals were not lofty. I didn't want to be President of the United States or conquer the world. My dream was to become a college professor. To educate myself to reach my dream, I needed income. I could not get any money from my parents, and because we were a middle class family, it was hard to get college grants and loans.

To generate income, I started up an insurance agency. I figured that if I wrote enough policies, I could have continual income from premiums—at least enough to support me through college. But as hard as I worked to get policies on the books, it was still hard to get paid. I was successful, but it just wasn't enough.

So I made two moves that changed my life permanently. First, inspired by the book *How I Took a Thousand Dollars and Made Five Million Investing in Real Estate* by William Nickerson, I turned to real estate. I borrowed money to buy my first couple of properties.

Second, simply out of the need to buy groceries for my family, I latched onto a job driving a taxicab. Have you ever had one of those experiences that afterwards continues to change just about everything else you do? Driving a taxi was just such an experience for me.

In order for you to understand what this is all about, you need to come back with me to my first day driving a cab. The company I started driving for, Yellow Cab Company in Tacoma, Washington, had a mandatory rule that entailed spending a day training with a cab driver-trainer named Bill Marsh.

After being out with Bill for about 45 minutes—30 minutes at Denny's getting him a cup of coffee—I realized that I could handle this cab driving business on my own. As I watched what he did, it dawned on me that to be a successful cab driver you only had to do one thing.

I asked Bill if he would take me back to the lobby to get my own taxi. He said I had to spend the whole "mandatory" day with him. "Look," I said. "could you please just take me back?"

Back at the cab company I talked to the owner/partner. "Mrs. Potter?" I said, "My name is Wade Cook. I'm a brand new cab driver. You don't know me, but is there any way I can just take a taxi out for the day?"

She replied, "Oh no, no. You have to spend the day with Bill Marsh."

I persisted. I explained to her that I knew Tacoma really well and told her that if she didn't like what I did by five or six o'clock that afternoon, she would never see me again. She listened and ended up giving me a little beat-up Dodge Dart for the day.

I took it out that first day and made $110—that was my net. The second day I came back with about $90 profits and the third day about $140. I was off and running. I began making between $3,200 and $3,800 a month. I needed about $1,200 a month to live on. I was able to take the rest, holding some out for taxes, and apply it to buying and fixing up houses. With this money, I purchased nine rental houses my first year. The rest of my real estate story is told in the books The *Real Estate Money Machine* and *How to Pick up Foreclosures*.

My point here is the lesson I learned in driving a taxi—to me the most significant and powerful financial lesson I have ever learned in my life. In fact, since then I've hobnobbed with some of the greatest financial minds in the country (doing radio, TV talk shows and seminars in 43 different states), and nothing I've learned from any of those men and women is more powerful than what I learned my first day driving a cab. The lesson is simply this—MONEY IS MADE IN THE METER DROP.

What does "the meter drop" mean? Every time you get into a taxi, the driver pushes the meter down (nowadays it's a computerized button), and it costs you $1.50 to $2. Whether it is a $5 run or a $50 run, you still pay $1.50 every time you get in the cab.

Many cab drivers only take big runs. In Tacoma they positioned themselves in town to get the run to Sea-Tac Airport, a $30-$35 fare. At the same time, I was beating the cab to death by going for all the small runs. I would take the $3, $6 and $8 runs. At the end of some busy days I would have up to forty, fifty or sixty runs. You see the difference? I was killing them. Now, don't get me wrong, I've had my share of big runs too. Sometimes a little $6 run would turn into a $15 run because the person my passenger was going to visit wasn't home. However, those extra meter jobs really added up to a lot of cash.

REPETITIVE CASH FLOW

This made it clear to me that the bottom line to wealth is duplication and repetition. A hamburger in Tampa Bay must taste just like a hamburger in San Francisco Bay, and McDonalds took advantage of this, not by selling one gigantic hamburger, but by selling billions of little ones—and french fries. Repetition made the McDonalds fortune.

About nine months after I started driving, Mrs. Potter called us all in for a meeting between shifts. While we were waiting for her to come in, all the cab drivers were bragging about how much money they were making. Bill Marsh sat there and said he had made more money in one month than anybody there. I casually asked him how much he made. With a note of triumph, he said, "One month I made $900." All the cab drivers started oohing over him, thinking that $900 was a lot of money.

Now remember, my lowest month was over $3,200. But I said with a smile, "Boy, that is a lot of money, Bill." No way was I going to mention to these guys how much I was making. They could see the rental properties I was buying and draw their own conclusions, but to this day, they still don't know.

On to real estate. At first, I did not follow the lesson I learned as a cabdriver. I went out and started the old buy-and-wait game. I waited for inflation, waited for Washington D.C. tax write-offs, and waited for other things I had no control over. After a year of playing the buy-and-wait game— the rental game—I had to sell one of my properties. I desperately needed money. I sold the property, received some cash for the down payment and carried back a mortgage. The key, however, is that I didn't get all cash up front. I sold the property under what you would call "owner financing."

I sat in my taxi, staring at the check I received from the down payment, and realized something: I had purchased this little property with $1,200 down; when I sold it, even after closing costs, I still ended up with $2,200—$1,000 more than I put into this property in the beginning. And, I would receive net monthly payments of $125 for 28 years.

I just stared at the check. I had stumbled across a whole new way of investing. I thought, why am I playing this buy-and-wait game? Why am I turning my life over to renters? Why wait for tax write-offs out of Washington D.C., hoping some benevolent congressman gets a depreciation bill passed through Congress? Why am I doing things I have no control over? Why don't I just go out and buy properties to sell? *Why not do the meter drop with my properties?*

I figured that I could sell a couple more rentals right away and then target properties I could buy and fix up a little bit, then turn around and sell on this "money machine."

Back then, I did not call it the "Money Machine." I called this "turning properties" or "flipping properties." Nevertheless, I realized that I had to treat real estate like the "meter drop." Instead of getting in and waiting, why not just buy for the sole purpose of reselling? This way I could build up a huge base of deeds of trust and mortgages and have monthly checks coming in. In the end it was these monthly checks that allowed me, and will allow you, to live the way we want.

At that time I had a lot of rental properties, but they were only making a little bit of money. If one renter didn't pay one month, it ruined the profits for the whole month. I was constantly putting more money into taking care of these properties. Any of you who have had rental properties realize that no matter what kind of money you have lying around in the bank, any rental property will "eat it up" and take it away from you. The giant "sucking sound" is real.

The rental game is just not what it is cracked up to be. However, the "Money Machine" is a fabulous way to make money by literally forcing the issue—rapidly accumulating wealth. I did this over the next year. I went out specifically looking for properties I could buy and sell quickly. Again, it was the meter drop. Get the passenger in, get the passenger out, and get on to the next deal. After doing many of these properties, I was able to quit and retire at the age of twenty-nine.

On To The Stock Market

Faced with time and financial freedom, I ended up writing a book. I never did go back to college to get my teaching degree, but I did end up with a book in the bookstores. Since that time, I have written several more. I entered the lecture circuit and started traveling the country. My semiretired state was really becoming a fun career. This also gave me the opportunity to make more money.

I knew I didn't want to put the excess money into savings accounts. I did buy a lot of second mortgages, which kept my cash flow ever increasing. In addition, $5,000 here and $10,000 there went into stock market investments.

I opened up a brokerage account and bought mutual funds, one of which had gone up in value 14% each of the previous three years. As soon as I bought it, it went down 2%. Quite a few stocks went up in value, but most of them floundered around and many went down. I figured the stock market was not for me, because I was going to have to learn a whole new set of rules and vocabulary to be successful at it. Meanwhile, I was still involved with real estate and teaching seminars.

Then I got a call from a friend who at that time was a stockbroker. He wanted to take me to lunch and explain what he was doing with many of his clients.

At lunch that day, I listened to a most fascinating idea, which struck a responsive chord telling me it was right and true, especially at that time. He wanted me to buy 100 shares of Motorola stock. (I don't do this with Motorola any more. The stock started to climb up to $100 a share and has since had a two-for-one split. The stock went back down to $50 and is now trading at around $70 a share. Maybe it will roll again, but I am just not sure.)

I bought 100 shares of Motorola at $50 a share for $5,000 plus $80 in commissions. The stockbroker asked me to put the stock up for sale at $60. Those of you who are familiar with the stock market and have brokerage accounts realize that you can put an order in to sell and take off for Hawaii. If, and when, the stock hits $60 a share, the sale will be triggered automatically by computer.

I put in the order to sell at $60 a share. About six weeks later, the stock hit $60 and the computer sold it. I had $6,000 in my account, minus about $90 in commissions. I made about $830 profit on this transaction. Then the stockbroker said to put in an order to buy the stock again at $50 a share. I put in an order for 108 shares at $50. About five weeks later the stock rolled backed down to $50 and the computer triggered a buy. Now I was the owner of 108 shares of Motorola at $50 a share.

At that time, the stock dropped down to around $48 or $49, and I was getting kind of worried. But it climbed right back up to $60 a share and the computer triggered a sale again. I had the excess profit in my account. The stock rolled from $50 to $60 a share several times and kept climbing up to $61–$62, so I did miss out on some of the profits. I did this particular stock many times for several years.

This cab driver had found a way to do a meter drop on Wall Street.

I contend that the stock market makes a perfect home-based business and/or a perfect place to develop extra income even if you are working or relying on an existing business. I am convinced that in every respect and aspect it is far superior to most other businesses. I have had a lot of businesses, from one-man shows to a large (in my estimation) 300+ employee corporation. Currently I am Director and President of Profit Financial Corporation—whose main subsidiary, United Support Association, Inc., is a powerhouse.

I have taken years to build the business and took it public in May of 1995. I only bring this up because I have employees, payroll taxes, advertising, and every other outlay of cash as well as concerns and considerations associated with running a large business. At times the "busyness" gets in the way of my true loves: family, teaching and working the brokerage accounts. I have tried to blend them together. I do owe an allegiance to my shareholders to be profitable. I have to make public how I work my stock and option deals in the corporate account. It is fun, profitable, and is building a tidy fortune for my immediate family (wife and children) and my shareholder family.

I realize that as I make a case for treating the stock market like a business, that I am competing with every "Amway" type company out there. My story is different though, because I am not inviting you to join my "downline." I want you to make a ton of bucks and keep ALL of them. I judge my success as an educator, not by how much I put into people but how much they get out of it. The business comparison can go a long way because you are probably familiar with most aspects (whether you are actually experienced or not) of running a business. Indeed, being familiar with what it takes to be successful may have caused you to get into business. We will dispel some falsehoods in a most unusual way. I will approach the comparison of using the stock market as a business by first stating the we are going to take a totally unconventional approach to creating a stock market income portfolio.

If you like mutual funds, or if you are happy with 6% to 10% annual returns, or if you are happy with the boring investments your stockbroker recommends, you probably should not read on. If you want some excitement, then join me as we turn the stock market into a business. I'll take a problem/solution approach:

Problem #1: Getting Started

Most small businesses require substantial up-front costs, to get up and going, and then to keep going until the business makes a profit. Usually the owner is the last to see the profit lining his pockets. Many times the owner goes into substantial debt just trying to get his or her business going.

Solution #1:

The Wade Cook method of investing in covered calls, rolling stock, stock options, dividends, spreads, buy-writes, rolling options, etc. requires as little as $500 to get going. These methods generate a quick profit—again, actual cash, which can be pulled out and used or be left alone to compound.

Most new businesses require a profound dedication and true commitment, and almost all businesses require extensive knowledge or experience. This brings me to problem number two.

Problem #2: Time/Financial Commitment

Businesses are like babies—especially at first. They demand attention. You have to be there. Even when and IF it grows, it requires more time to train and trust managers. It is hard to take vacations. It is difficult, but not impossible, to have a family life and/or a church life.

Solution #2:

The stock market, again the Wade Cook way, allows you to be as involved as you want. Most investors definitely "work" part-time. You control your time.

When I am teaching at one of my seminars, I start with this question—"How many of you want to make over $100,000 per year?" Hands shoot up all over the classroom. Then I ask, "If you want to make over $100,000 per year, why are you talking to anyone about making money who is making less than that?" And then I continue, "To whom are you listening? Where are you getting your advice?"

You can probably relate to this question. You have probably kicked yourself for following the financial advice of people who "ain't makin' no money." Ironically, when you finish reading my chapters, you will probably ask some stockbroker (maybe even a well-known broker) whether you should buy my books and attend a Wall Street Workshop. He or she will probably give you unintelligent advice. Just let him or her read the guarantee that I provide on the back of every one of my brochures, and be assured that because of my guarantee, you have nothing to lose and everything to gain. Please note, many of my students are stockbrokers who sit dazed and amazed at their former naivete. These students may have known bits and pieces before attending one of my Wall Street Workshops, but no one, and I mean NO ONE, has ever shown them how to systematically use a formula to generate perpetual income.

Your participation in your stock market business is only a few minutes at a time. You can read and study in your spare time, (on airplanes, at lunch, in the bathroom, etc.) A minimal amount of knowledge can be leveraged repetitiously to generate outstanding income. And you do not need a host of employees or managers to help you.

Problem #3: Overhead

With a traditional business you have rent, insurance, equipment, employees, taxes (FICA, employee withholding), phones, computers, even pencils and every other imaginable and unimaginable expense. The relentlessness of these expenses make it difficult to make a profit on a continued basis. And it seems the amount of money needed to cover expenses rises to use up any available cash you have.

Solution #3:

This is where your business is very different. Simply put, you have none of these. Once you learn the Wade Cook formulas, you only buy stock or options and then sell them to generate a profit. If you currently have a brokerage account, it is easy to start investing, and there are many ways to make a profit (selling covered calls, selling puts, rolling options, etc.) without having any overhead. When you make a profit, you keep it all. There aren't a dozen strainers or filters for your profits to go through, each one decreasing its size along the way, and all this before you get paid.

After two or three months of implementing these easy-to-use, but profound methods, most business entrepreneurs will be ecstatic. I know you will love the simplicity of it all.

Problem #4: Capitalizing Your Business

Most businesses require a lot of start up money for buildings (rent, lease, purchase) product development, equipment, operating expenses, etc. They also require a large investment of time and energy, and most have a revenue curve which can take 6 months to 2 years to show any profit.

Solution #4A:

You can start in the stock market with almost nothing. Granted, if you start with less than a thousand dollars, it is more difficult because the commissions eat up a large part of your smaller profits. But you surely don't need the amount of capital required to start up a traditional business.

Solution #4B:

Line of credit. I realize this part will not solve all your starting needs but "Margin Investing" is fun and it is definitely available. When you put $5,000 into your brokerage

An Immediate Line Of Credit Is Available.

firm, your broker will let you borrow an additional $5,000 to buy stocks.

This is a loan and the broker gets to choose the collateral (stocks they take). They will also charge interest on the outstanding balance (this is peanuts compared to the profits which can be generated).

You should be careful and pick stocks on dips, or stocks which will improve (use this amount for writing covered calls). If you make 22% to 38% per month, 7% to 9% interest a year is a small price to pay. See margin variations and concerns in the *Wall Street Money Machine*.

The solution to the second point listed above provides an interesting twist. Not only can you start your stock market cash flow business part time (even minutes a day), you can do this even when your existing business demands a lot of you. I use my car phone a lot. It allows me to be effective on the road and even when I travel.

Other interesting points:

1) Most people go into business for many reasons besides making money. They want to expand and grow, they want to develop and produce an idea, a product, or a service, and they want to not only control their destiny long-term, but their time on a daily basis. Once in business they realize their time is controlled by other people and other things. They realize too late that most of their efforts are directed in ways which produce very little of their actual profits.

    They are quite delighted when they experience the simplicity of the methods of interfacing with the stock market (usually a phone call to their broker), the quick profits, and the end of the things that slow down the movement of income to the bottom line.

2) Investors can read and do research in the oddest places; driving around, in airplanes, while waiting, etc.

3) Investors can easily turn a getaway into a working vacation. Yes, you may need time away from your main business or job, but a few minutes here and there can really build up your stock market cash flow. 15 minutes a day could pay for your whole vacation and then some.

Problem #5: Specialized Knowledge

While it's true in your own business that you need a product or service and a certain degree of expertise in them, it's not exactly true in running your brokerage account.

Solution #5:

1) Once you understand the Wade Cook system, learning and using specific formulas for cash flow generation, then you don't have to know everything about computer chips to invest in high tech stocks, or in temporary help companies to invest in them, etc. You learn the simple formulas and repetitions, and find companies which fit. Your expertise is in the methods—working the formula.

2) As you start to invest for holding purposes—building your retirement portfolio, you can then get to be an expert in finding companies which are experts (specialists) in their own fields. You'll learn a lot about yields, what drives a stock, book value, earnings ratios, etc., as you move to this point.

Note: I realize that someone hearing this for the first time may not understand this, so a very brief explanation is in order. I, Wade Cook, believe that at first an investor should employ a very aggressive approach to income generation. Proxy (options) investing allows an investor, by starting with a few thousand dollars, to build up to several hundred thousand in a year or two. I have too many students to count who have done this. It's exciting. Later you can take some profits, continue to do aggressive plays, but buy stocks which you like for the long haul. You can also take some profits and move them away from the market to buy real estate, second mortgages, CD's, annuities, etc. These have their own risk factors, but you are diversified.

3) If you have your own business, you probably know what it takes to be profitable, to expand and grow. This same knowledge can help you find in other companies the characteristics for success. For example: If you're a start up, you should know what it takes: look for Initial Public Offerings (IPO's). If you've run your own business this will make sense. Use it to your best advantage.

Before I move off this topic, let me share a few more ideas.

Most businesses fail. Something like 80% of all new start-ups fail their first year. Of the 20% that make it, 80% of those fail the second year. That's a net of 4 or 5 businesses which make it. However, in franchising, 85% of franchisees make it their first year. Why? They have a track to run on, service and support, experience of the franchisor, combining the synergistic expertise of other franchisees, manuals, etc. The franchise fee and on-going fees are small prices to pay for good backup and support.

Wade Cook Seminars (a division of Profit Financial Corporation) has training, backup support, a clearinghouse of ideas, etc. to help small investors, real estate investors, and small business people make a dramatic impact on their bottom line. If you don't use our training, please get it somewhere. Your first and then your continued and paramount investment should be in knowledge.

Problem #6: Wealth Problems

Once you start making good money you become a target for higher taxes, lawsuits and other risks.

Solutions #6:

Problem A: You need to learn how to reduce your exposure to risk and liability.

Solution A: Set up a Nevada Corporation, Family Limited Partnership, and Business Trust.

Problem B: You need to pay fewer taxes.

Solution B: Attend Wade Cook Seminar's **Wealth Academy**. Set up a Nevada Corporation (even have a brokerage account in another state), a Charitable Remainder Trust, and a Pension Plan.

Problem C: Make sure your family and church get everything.

Solution C: Use a Quality Family Living Trust in conjunction with other entities like a Charitable Remainder Trust (CRT).

NOTE: Call Wade Cook Seminars and ask about the B.E.S.T. (Business and Entity Skills Training which accompanies the Wall Street Workshop) and Wade Cook Seminar's flagship event—the WEALTH ACADEMY. 1-800-872-7411.

THE PROPER BLENDING OF THESE ENTITIES
TRULY BRINGS PEACE OF MIND

Problem #7: Retiring at Age 35 or Being Really Cash Flow Rich at 65

Solution #7:

Treat the stock market like a business. Buy wholesale, sell retail. Only buy so that you have something to sell. Be aggressive. The preceding methods are what my books and seminars are all about. Many people, starting with even $10,000 are ready to totally retire a year or two later. This is no joke. I say ready because they could if they wanted to but they're having too much fun. If you know you're going to make $5,000 today, it's pretty easy to get out of bed.

1) Do you invest in a Pension type account?
   A. Keogh Plan for self employed,
   B. A Corporate Pension Plan,
   C. An IRA, SEP IRA or the like.

Use peripheral entities for conducting the business or investments.

2) Many investments are "retirement" in nature.
   A. Annuities
   B. Real Estate
   C. Section 29, 42, Tax Advantaged Investments
All are deferred until you sell.

Training will help you determine which is right and when it's right for you!

When a person is starting a business or in the midst of running or building up a business, his or her time demands are onerous.

Treating pension money like a business—doing aggressive strategies may be next to impossible. It may be difficult even putting money aside.

Two thoughts:

1) Do it anyway. Two-step the money away from your business. Discipline yourself to put money aside—the highest percentage (amount) possible even if you have to let it sit for awhile—invested in passive, "no hassle" investments.

2) Later when you slow down the "busyness" part of your life, then get more aggressive with your retirement money. Once you see how fast it compounds tax free, you'll wish you had started earlier. The point: Get rich in an account (entity) which pays no taxes. Don't put this off.

Remember you get a "double benefit" when you use a pension type arrangement.

1) Tax deductible donations—INVESTING WITH BE-FORE-TAX MONEY

2) ALL income (dividends, interest, partnership, etc.) and all capital gains are made tax free and compound tax FREE.

THAT'S RIGHT, TAX FREE—the pension plan pays no taxes. You only have to claim income in 30 to 40 years when you pull it out.

Problem #8: Include Family/Train Kids

An age old problem exists in not only trying to involve your family but also in making sure they can perpetuate the dynasty.

Solution #8:

You'll have just as much problem here as in any business. Care, concern, legality, and dedication are time honored problems.

A) A few solutions:

1) Let your children manage (a fictitious) account at first. Later let them play with real money.

2) Put money into an IRA for your kids to manage.

3) Let them slowly take over the family accounts. (Set up so they can only trade—not make withdrawals.)

4) Let kids earn their way through college.

5) Discuss strategies frequently, assign them research projects.

6) Have them visit companies and ask questions.

7) Immerse them in reading—articles, stories, reports, news releases.

8) Plan working vacations—visit factories, companies (many will give tours).

9) Attend shareholder meetings.

10) Track the impact of:
    a) new products and services
    b) competition
    c) expansion
    d) acquisition of debt
    e) other news

11) Take them to seminars, forums, etc. Call Wade Cook Seminars about the Youth Wall Street Workshop.

12) Listen to them. Let them in to ask their questions and let their questions guide you.

B) More thoughts for older kids:

I believe the best financial gift a mother and father can leave is instilling in their children a desire to be self-sufficient, a team player, passionate and willing to do "what it takes" to support their families. If the parents are rich and have older children, they eventually need to be brought into the family dynasty—either to dismantle it or perpetuate it. All of the thoughts given above for younger children apply to your 40 and 60 year old children—most adults are teenagers when it comes to wealth protection and wealth endowment.

Problem #9: Winding Down Your Business

Sometimes it is more difficult to end a business than it is to start. You may have employees, leases, contracts, and commitments. It can be painful.

Solution #9:

Stock Market investing has no such demands. The worst "hard to get out of" situation you could get into would be a stock or mutual fund which is currently down in value.

Some thoughts:

1) If you follow the Wade Cook System your emphasis will have been on cash flow. Retiring will mean doing less or putting your extensive profits into high yielding investments or Section 29 income and utility stocks, bonds, MIPS, etc. for income and tax credits.

2) The activity of building your fortunes will now help you choose wise investments. If you have been using careful forethought, you will have used some of your profits to have purchased high quality stocks. Quitting will not be painful but a smooth transition many months or years in the making. You will learn how to build a solid Financial House with a good supporting foundation.

Problem #10: Drive and Passion—Fun and Excitement

Rarely have I seen a true entrepreneur go into business for the "money" alone. They want to help to contribute to others and to better their family's position. Most humans know instinctively that the way to wealth is to enlarge the pie. The problem is many get bogged down, dismayed and even after decades feel unsatisfied.

Solution #10:

The stock market will not solve this last problem. The proper application of knowledge is exciting. Working and fine-tuning cash flow formulas will produce pronounced results. Involving family and friends can be gratifying. Preparing for a great retirement is thrilling. Planning your financial affairs so your family, church, or charity get everything is satisfying. Ultimately, your true happiness will come down to your relationship between you and your Maker

It is to this ultimate end that we at Wade Cook Seminars dedicate our service to you and hope that we are but one stepping stone to help your sojourn on this earth be one of peace, happiness and fulfillment.

3

EARNING MONEY

That portion of your portfolio you've chosen to use as your cash generation machine should be used wisely, yet aggressively as you see fit.

It is in your comfort level that you will trade. As you gain more experience, you'll probably spread the edge of the envelope—try new things, or variations. This chapter is about several of these other ways of making money. However, in order to put this information in such a way you can easily use it, this chapter is like a "play sheet," or a checklist. It will cover most of my formulas in an abbreviated format. I'll try to be complete with the quantity, but brief with the explanation. Indeed, I'll try to keep the definition or explanation to one or two paragraphs.

Each of these formulas is explained in detail in other books, primarily the *Wall Street Money Machine*, other home study courses, primarily *Zero to Zillions*, and in other reports I write as I perfect various strategies.

I wish more than anything that when I started investing I would have had a chapter like this — to see in a few pages all the potential plays, formulas and recipes.

So here we go. We'll start with my old favorite. Remember, these strategies are about generating predictable cash flow.

ROLLING STOCK

There are certain stocks which trade within a certain range. Some brokers call this channeling. They move up to a high (resistance) and then to a low (support). Many stocks do this, but the ones I like (so I don't have a lot of cash tied up) are cheaper stocks—say in the $1 to $5 range. I find a stock which goes from $2 to $2.75. It doesn't seem like a lot of profit, but 75¢ on a $2 investment in one to three or four months is not bad. Look at the following examples:

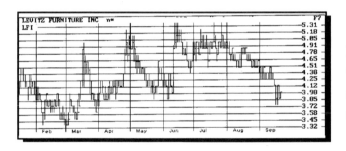

You can see Levitz trading between $ 4 and $5 about every month or so.

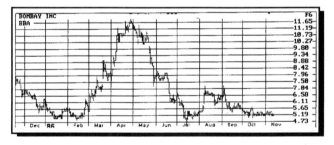

Bombay has been rolling between $5 and $7.

The three rules of rolling stocks are:

(1) You always know your exit before you go in the entrance.

(2) Don't get greedy—sell below the high for quicker and surer profits.

(3) Stick with the less expensive stocks—so you can buy more.

Many high-priced stocks roll. Look at the following:

These are nice predictable rolls, but they are high priced. I play them, but with options. See the section on Rolling Options. (For more information on a rolling stock, see *Wall Street Money Machine* and *Zero To Zillions,* and of course, the *Live Wall Street Workshop.*)

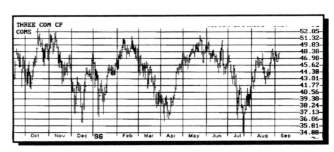

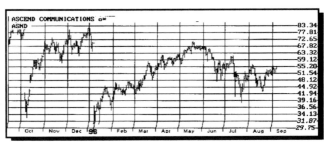

BOTTOM FISHING

This is a simple way of finding stocks which are severely underpriced, or at least ones which you think have a high likelihood for going much higher.

Stocks in this category could come from:

- Really bad news.

- Bankrupt (Chapter 11) companies on their way out of bankruptcy.

- Turnarounds.

- Companies just going public or just getting listed on an exchange.

- Companies breaking out of their roll range with better earnings, new products, etc.

- Traditional penny stocks with some reason (pressure) for the stock to go up.

I do bottom fishing stocks all the time. I bought 141,500 shares of one company at around $.06 and sold it 18 months later for $1.40 to $1.50. A nice $200,000 plus profit! I look for more opportunities like this all the time.

DIVIDENDS

I also like to share in the profits of the company. I take all the dividends I can take, but for the most part I'd rather the company keep the profits and expand the business.

These dividends include regular dividends, irregular dividends (which I look for all the time), a cash distribution (which may not be taxable, but which reduces the price of the stock which could be sold for a loss), and MIPS, or monthly income preferred securities—large companies which pay out monthly checks.

One of my strategies is to own the stock long enough (sometimes as little as one day) to capture the dividend. Wait until it increases in value, then sell it. I do this every quarter with certain stocks.

OPTIONS

Buying stock options gives the investor a chance to control large amounts of stocks with a small amount of money. An option gives you the right (not the obligation) to buy or sell a stock. Because options end—they expire—they are very risky. If you learn how to play them well, the profits can be phenomenal. I've written extensively on many forms of options investing elsewhere, so only a brief synopsis is here.

CALL OPTIONS: A right to buy stock. You buy these when you think the stock is going up. This could be on a SLAM (serious down movement), a roll, (when the stock is at the bottom of the roll range), or a stock with good news, etc. In short, when you think the stock has pressure to move up, buy a call, ride it up, and sell.

PUT OPTIONS: A right to sell stock. You build value in your put option as the stock decreases. Buy puts when the stock hits a high, or is at the top of its roll range, in short, when you think the high price can't be sustained.

ROLLING OPTIONS: Buying calls or selling puts when a stock is at its low range and then buying a put, or selling a call, when it peaks out and starts back down. Look at the following:

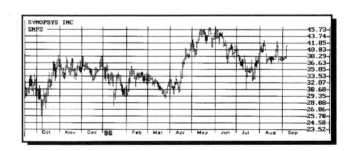

This gives you a way to make money on both sides of the movement.

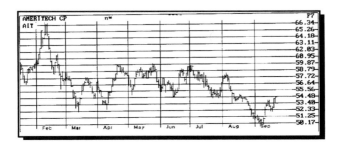

SELL CALLS—COVERED: Writing covered calls is perhaps my favorite way to generate consistent cash flow. Yes, there are other ways I make more money, but not as consistently. This method lets you generate income (in one day) by selling a call option on stock you already own or stock you've purchased for just this purpose.

The rules include:

(1) Buying stock on margin—this allows you to double your rate of return.

(2) Volatility—almost like a rolling stock so we can take advantage of the swings.

(3) Keeping within the $5 to $25 price range for maximum returns with a small amount of cash tied up.

There are many variations, techniques, and examples found in my other books.

As the stock moves down, the price of the options moves down also. In writing covered calls, we either sell the call (uncovered—if we don't own the stock) or buy the stock (hopefully at the low) and wait to sell the call as the stock increases. We want maximum cash flow so we sell at the "maximum" time.

We bought the stock at $4 and sold the $5 call (about 35 days away—the next month) for $1.25 when the stock was $4.87. At the time we bought the stock, the $5 call was 12.5¢. We take advantage of the stock movement, hence compounding the option rate of return.

UNCOVERED CALLS: Many of you won't be able to do this until you have more experience or more cash in your account. This is called "going naked," in that you don't own the stock. You use this strategy when the stock is at the high part of its range. You sell the call—generating pure cash. You wait. As the stock moves down, your obligation to deliver (sell) the stock goes down and eventu-ally disappears as the time expires. You made money with no invest-ment. The risk is that if the stock goes up, you'll have to buy it at a higher price (offset by the cash you made for selling the call). Don't sell calls on stocks you think are going up; either buy the stock low (covered) and wait to sell the call—getting a higher premium for the options and eventually selling

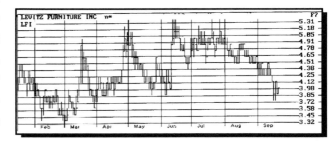

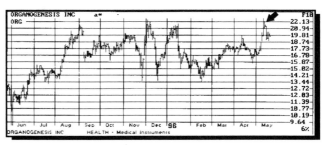

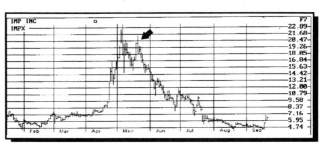

(getting called out) at a higher price, or sell the call when the stock is high—wait for a dip and then:

a) buy the stock or

b) buy back the option or

c) just let the option expire and keep the cash!

SELLING PUTS: This is a great way to make money. You sell a put, generating income. You are selling the right for someone to put (sell) the stock to you at a fixed price. You use this strategy when the stock is low and heading up. The income (premium) you received is yours to keep. As the stock rises, the put option you sold goes down in value. You could either buy back the option at a lower price and keep the difference, or let it lapse on the expiration date. If the stock has risen above the strike price, no one will put it to you. If you do have to buy the stock, the cost is offset by the premium received—like buying wholesale.

TANDEM PLAYS: There are many combinations, but my favorite is a combination of buying/selling calls and buying/selling puts. Here is how it works (See the chapter : "Tandem Plays" for more on this).

When the stock is low, sell a put and buy a call—both strategies gain advantage with an increase in the stock price. You make money now selling the put and you make more later selling the call option you purchased.

When the stock is high, sell a call and buy a put. You make money on each as the stock moves down. This gives you four plays on a rolling stock with options.

SHORT SELLING: Short selling allows you to borrow stock, sell it and generate income. As the stock moves down, you purchase it, pay off the loan (borrowed stock) and pocket the difference. Its easier said than done, but in my case, I'd rather buy puts if I think the stock is going down. I use short selling when I've sold a naked call and have to perform. I'll borrow stock to cover my position and hope it turns down.

BLUE CHIPS: There are so many definitions of blue chips that you need to make up your own definition. These are the stocks you want to own for a long time. They could be brand name stocks, large companies that have fallen out

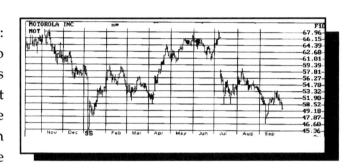

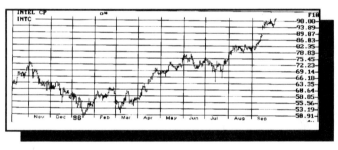

of favor, even regional companies you can identify with.

CASH FLOW

Use your profits from selling stocks/options for investing in real estate or other investments like businesses or put your money into good, solid, Blue Chips. The name of the game is to get your stock market profit buying your "hold" investments.

You choose the percentages of your money that work best for you. This is a good solid growth.

4

QUICK TURN PROFITS

CAPITALIZING PROFITS

I wrote my first book almost two decades ago. I have had a wonderful audience —a very supportive following. Those of you who know how I write and how I think will definitely be unsettled by the following chapter!

There is a purpose, a rhyme and reason to my madness. Indeed, it is in my attempt to explain my "stock market madness" that the following is written. Why? People come up and ask me how I can make such fantastic returns. How do I consistently get 10,000% plus annualized returns?

So come along—I hope you'll come to understand my rationale and my results. It will take a while, but the first part of this chapter is necessary to understand the last part, the crucial part. It may be slow at first, and you'll have to wade through my "Wade-isms," as I have never before tried to encapsulate my thinking process and results. This is new territory. Hopefully not the final frontier.

HOLY MACRO

I hope to give a "macro-view" and use micro examples to justify my reasoning. There definitely is a "herd" mentality and I am not the first one to try to understand it and to figure out how to profit from it, or how to not lose by following it. More importantly, trying to understand this type of stock market mentality is the perfect way to try to figure out just when the "herd" is about to turn. This turning point is the point when a lot of profits can be made. But I'm ahead of myself. That is the conclusion to this chapter. The profit-making point of reversal or correction of a stock is crucial. I bring it up at the beginning so you know where this chapter is heading. I will not be untrue to the theme that has worked well for me, both in my personal investing and my seminars: Use a little cash to purchase an asset, get in, then get out with a nice chunk of cash (profits) or smaller cash flows (payments). In short, I want income (cash flow) from dividends, capital gains, option premiums, or whatever income that allows us to live, to pay the bills, and grow rich.

Another theme of my books and seminars is "to whom are we listening?" If you want to make $100,000 a year, why are you listening to anyone making under $100,000 a year? It is to this point that we'll launch into this area of discussion.

There is a widespread belief that the market is always right. I disagree. There are too many variables. The market is not always right. When it comes to a particular stock, there is definitely too much sentiment to come to any conclusion that a stock's price is "right." (I'll give in on this a little, if you're determining a stock price based on a "best guess" midpoint price between a high and a low, or a recent support level and resistance level.)

I'll get back to individual stocks later, but for now let's deal with the stock market in general.

COMMON BELIEFS

Supply and Demand. There is a common "wish" that all things be simple. And even if complicated, at least that they be explainable and definable. Do markets move due to a supply and a demand? Yes, to an extent, but there is too much sentiment, too many desires, and far too many biases which come into play.

MARKET SENTIMENT

When you have sentimental responses to hard facts, you are bound to get a distortion. Those who believe in equilibrium or that the market is a zero-sum game are often fooled. A Fund Manager may make a clever play one day, but then be hoisted on his own petard the next.

Market sentiment is a combination of multiple dynamics at work. If we were to achieve perfect knowledge, have perfect competition, and perfect responses to all this, and more importantly, if we could be detached from the game, then maybe we could pre-guess a movement. But we get nothing perfect and we are not detached. Indeed, we are a part of the course of events.

When we buy stocks, we're part of the process that drives the stock up; when we sell, we are the opposite. The amount of stock movement depends on where the market is headed—what stage, or cycle it is in.

INFLUENCE

We, individually, have little influence, but collectively we have a lot. If we are in the game, buying a stock or many stocks, we contribute. We become part of the trend. We want safety so we go with the numbers—the "herd."

This has never made sense to me—as most of the stock market makes no sense to me. I love "crazy!" Since I accumulate wealth through chaos—at least, figuring out part of the chaos and capturing profits amidst it, and since I don't have to continue in the trend, in fact I can be detached from it (as you can)—then you and I can make incredible returns.

MR. SPOCK, WHERE ARE YOU?

If you think the stock market is logical, or that a certain move in a particular stock price is logical, then I will show you dozens of illogical moves! Can you predict a price change—100% of the time? No. Can you do your best to make a calculated risk? Yes.

Try this one on for size. When a stock price starts to rise, it creates excitement. The higher it goes (or the faster the rise) the more investors want in on the action. It rises more. More investors buy in. It rises and rises, sometimes 10% to 20% in a few days. Then . . . it stops! Does it just stay there? Or does it swing back down? Usually it falls, as investors' sentiment takes it the other way.

I'll give a 5-step process in a while, but first, what is happening here? Which price was right—the price two weeks ago at $80 a share, or the price now at $120. And three weeks from now, what will be right? The $90 price which the stock has fallen back to, or the $80 or high of $120?

What did supply and demand have to do with this? What about the market always being right, or a search for equilibrium, or any other high-falutin' theory exposed by a guru of

Wall Street? Maybe, just maybe, this $30 run up was because a competitor's Indonesia mining operation turned sour. But look what the "herd" did!

Here's another one. Throughout this past year employment reports have been good—more people employed. To me this should be good news. It means more people working, paying taxes, and not living off the government. It means more savings, more spending and all the other great things that help make a bigger American pie.

But, no. The stock market (DJIA) falls 80 points. Why? Because, as those wonderful things happen, inflation will go up, then the Feds, in 9 months or a year, will edge up interest rates; corporate profits will decline slightly in 12 to 18 months, so the stocks price will fall. But they fall now in anticipation of this chain of events—which no one can predict anyway.

I rest my case for craziness. However, this last point does make a nice segue to a discussion of future events.

PERFECTING THE FUTURE

Markets rise and fall on a perception of what will happen in the future. I have two problems with this.

(1) No one knows what will happen. Too many other things change. What seems logical turns illogical.

(2) We still must take into account our biases—how we as individuals and groups view such things. Life is too fluid to predict.

Most of the future's news is discounted long before it happens. Look at the last example! We want to discern things, to have peace of mind, to have things fit—to make sense. What twisted logical path did the market (the invisible "they") walk down to come to a conclusion that a stock's price will fall in nine to eighteen months, and then have the price fall now? With this type of logic at work and the crazy reaction to it, what are we to do? More importantly, what plays can we make to build up our income?

I'll give specifics in a few moments, but first, my list of important observations:

A. Individual Investors

    (1) There is in each of us (even at the corporate level) a desire to grow, to build, to achieve.

    (2) We all, even companies, have a desperate need to not only survive, but to thrive.

B. Market Movement

    (1) The market has a mind of its own and will usually do that which it must do to make fools out of a majority of investors.

    (2) The market is not right. It just isn't. It's fluid, it moves unexpectedly.

    (3) There are short term plays and long-term plays—you decide the length of time.

    (4) There are opportunities everywhere.

    (5) Investors' actions shape future events, not predict them. They cause change, not reflect it.

    (6) Investor bias rationalizes (and hence changes) the facts.

(7) You can profit going both ways—up prices, down prices.

(8) The "herd" mentality takes over and when it's played out (the boom), then prices start down as they bottom out (the bust), then the cycle starts over.

(9) It is at this precise moment when you capitalize on profits.

That took a lot to get to these points, so let's keep rolling. Let's use a stock moving up for whatever reason as our example. We own a stock or have an option on it. The stock moves with a mind of its own. It's reflective of news—good earnings, higher dividend paid out, prospects for the next few years. Everyone wants in. The price

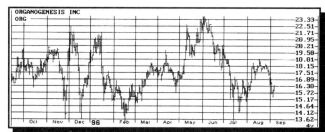

goes up and up. However, it will turn around to some degree. The sentiment will change.

The time comes when the momentum will turn. Perhaps the turn will come when an analyst at a major firm, a person who has loved this stock (to death!), now thinks it shouldn't be an "aggressive buy," but a "buy," or a "hold." A small downgrade. If you are into buying puts or going short on the stock, wouldn't it be great to sell at the peak, or buy the puts just as it's about to fall?

This is it. Playing this high point and the corresponding reverse (bottom) is point for action. And, it's just not that tough to make money this way. We'll call this point a "crossover," or a convergence. Crossovers occur at both peaks and valleys.

We'll explore this premise after we look at a scenario. This scenario conforms to this strategy. Not all scenarios do, but the ones which do, allow us to get in, then get out with a lot of cash. This scenario plays out frequently, I'm not investing in "the market" but in certain stocks and options within the general market. And if you think the market has a mind of its own , go with the trend. Don't try to "catch a falling piano." But only go so far.

FIVE SECTIONS (STAGES) OF A CROSSOVER (THE BOOM/BUST SCENARIO)

FIRST: The price movement is unnoticeable. The trend starts, the price rises or falls inordinately quickly, compared to its historical moves. Volume increases as stock momentum builds. Look at the following:

Speed Way Motorsports (TRK)

December 1995, stock had been trading between $25 and $30 for the last four months with no big trend. Volume (interest) in TRK increased in December of 1995 and January of 1996 and

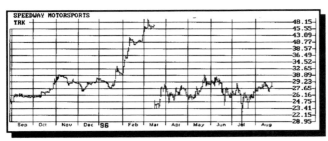

the stock started to climb. The stock split in mid March and has been trading between $25 and $30 for the last six months.

K-Mart (KM)

K - M a r t
showed a building
trend in Septem-
ber and October
of 1995, with a big
trend up in early
1996. K-Mart
then showed

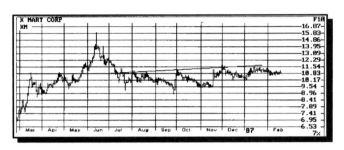

trend reversal from December of 1995 to February of 1996. As
the stock was falling, so was the volume. The stock changed
trend in March,
volume in-
creased and so
did the stock
price.

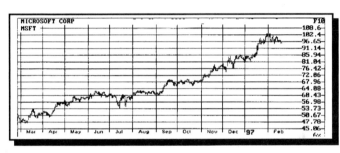

SECOND:
Activity rein-
forces more ac-
tivity. Recommendations (from the professionals) fly. Everyone wants in. Ma-
jor purchases oc-
cur.

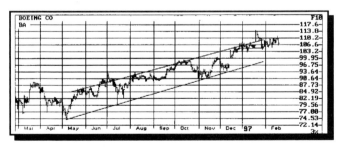

THIRD: The
strength (or
weakness) is
tested. Doubts
occur in the wis-
dom of the recommendation. New recommendations appear,
after all the facts are used, distorted and abused to prove
points.

FOURTH: The main point, or question, is simple—is the price sustainable?

    (1) Where is the market headed?

    (2) Check other news.

    (3) How was the news received?

    (4) How much buying has been going on?

    (5) How many institutions jumped in?

    (6) When the high and low was tested, did the price return to the previous support level or did it break support?

FIFTH: Divergence. If there is no compelling reason for it to stay high, it will decline. BUT IF THERE IS NO COMPELLING REASON FOR A FALL, it may fluctuate, but the stock might establish a new range. The price will be tested repeatedly. The opposite is true for a falling stock, once it hits bottom. The bottom support level will be tested repeatedly.

A PERSPECTIVE

Go with the "herd" until the time is right. Buck the trend at that time. I have seen very rapid movements up and down. I hope after this next sentence or two, my strategy will make sense. So much doesn't make sense, but this does. The stock price will change.

If I own a stock at $80 and it gets trendy—caught in an updraft, I'd rather sell at $110—even if it goes to $120, because in two hours it could fall to $90, or a $50 stock could fall to $35 (IOM). *A good time to get out would be when you wouldn't get in.*

UP ELEVATORS/DOWN ELEVATORS

Here is a micro point on these movements. I think good news plays out in days. However, it can take months for company's stock prices to recover from bad news.

Now, if you're playing the stock, either long or short, the length of time is crucial to your profitability. However, if you're playing stock options, a high point and then small percentage down in the stock, or a bottom and small recovery in the stock ($1 to $5) could produce drastic profits.

DEFINE A JOKE

Watching "Data" on Star Trek is a lesson in human behavior. Laughing (getting a joke) is difficult—at least the timing is difficult. Data doesn't get jokes. He can't tell one, or understand the punchline. I saw a bad movie (Solo) and the humanoid (machine) questioned why everyone was laughing. "A joke," he was told. Obviously, he wants to know what a joke is. No good explanation was given. Let me try my hand at it. I'll then get back to booms and busts. A joke is a story, and at the end a complete surprise occurs, either in the actions of the participants, or a twist in words, with unexpected meaning, hidden meaning, or a nuance to something else. Based on your point of reference, the company you're in, or the mood you're in, determines your response—a chuckle, a scoff or a belly laugh, etc.

It is the twist, or reversal that interests me. Never has a movie brought tears to my eyes as the end of Steel Magnolias—then in a half second, everyone is busting a gut laughing. The writer played our emotions like a maestro. The markets also thrive on fear and greed, and unexpected reversals.

CHANGE IS INEVITABLE

When stocks move up or down—either unexpectedly or in reaction to news, especially if they move quickly, there is a high incidence of a major divergence. A favorite play is to buy a call on the low-side turnaround, and buy a put on the top-side turnaround.

I've gone from the macro and philosophical point of view to the micro and practical application. I make hundreds of thousands of dollars (and my students make more) using this simple (I hope it's still simple) strategy. I make money on the MICRO plays. You need constant surveillance to buck the trend and break from the herd.

A perception of the facts (right or wrong), starts the movement. Activity breeds activity and more investors rush in. They listen to current events and future predictions and that subsequently affects the price. Their purchasing/selling is integral to the process. New information—either right or wrong tests the strength or weakness of the previous assumption/activity, and the price is sustained or divergence occurs. A short term profit can be made. It's quick and semi-predictable. Get in and out before anyone ever sees (or reacts to) the trend.

Now, use your profits to increase your holdings in great companies. It is the very *boom and bust cycle* (volatility) which gets me excited. Most investors run from the boom and bust scenario, however, some of us profit big time from this technique.

5

FUN-DAMENTALS

CHOOSING STOCK WISELY

If there is a way to make the selection of a stock and building a portfolio of solid stocks a fun process, we'll make every attempt to find it. A few assumptions: 1) We want to find stocks at bargain prices, and 2) we surely do not want to overpay for our stocks.

Isn't that the essence of it all—to find great stocks at bargain prices? Also, we want to buy stock with the highest likelihood of increases in value and the lowest likelihood of losing value. If the stock produces a dividend (income) that would be nice too.

REAL ESTATE: A FOUNDATIONAL EXAMPLE

Determining value is very perplexing and very difficult. Over the years many ways of determining value have been proposed. Whether we're buying or selling, we want the best price. The three most common ways to determine real estate value are listed here. After this short exploration we'll use what's applicable from this to aid us in choosing stocks.

1) Cost or Replacement Value

Buildings and land have value based on how it is being used. We'll explore more of this in the income section, but we'll cover it briefly here. A building used as a factory will be worth so much: use it for residences and it may go up in value. Turn it into a shopping center and it goes up again. You can't do this with stock, but what the company does with its assets can change what it's worth.

With real estate we just figure what it costs to replace the building—including the land—and that's the replacement cost. Is it this simple? Well—not quite.

2) Income

The gross and net income and the use of income multipliers are the most commonly used basis for the determination of value. You see, the cost of replacing a structure is not adequate to determine the full or accurate value.

What income does a building make? And even if you know that to the penny, other factors enter in:

A) How long has it been since a rent increase?

B) How expensive is the debt? And can it be refinanced or paid off?

C) Can other expenses be lowered?

And none of this has to do with the tax deductions. How does it affect our tax bracket? All sorts of other variations occur. If we raise the rents, will the income remain stable? If we "net" more, the value will increase—could it be refinanced at a higher price and the new-found money used to buy more properties?

3) "Comps"

One common way to value real estate is to find properties in the area which have sold recently and determine the value of your property based on an average of several properties— taking into account the differences. This is one of the functions of appraisers. Banks use this method extensively so they are not giving mortgages above "what the neighborhood will bear." Extensive appraisals can be done using all three of these methods. It is wise to use all three with a more nebulous "growth potential" factor thrown in. The potential for growth or increase in value is a reason why many real estate investors invest in the first place, but so many things change, and there are so many chances to be wrong, that hardly anyone uses it as a main factor in determining current value.

I could go on, but since this is a chapter about stocks, let's just take from real estate the thought behind the process. The example of real estate cannot solve all the problems, or answer all the questions, but it is worthwhile. It's good to have another point of reference. I'm good at many of my stock decisions because I integrate knowledge I gained in real estate.

The point is not that many companies own real estate, but that the price of the stock, the income, and tax consequences have many similar characteristics.

Now, To Stocks

There are five major areas to look at in determining the value of the stock. There are several minor aspects and variations which can also be examined. No one of these should stand alone. You will get a "blind men and the elephant" view if you do so. Also, there is no set "weighting" exercise which I've found. In the end it comes down to your feelings and the risk you're willing to take; the direction you want to go.

Fundamental analysis is different than technical analysis. Technical analysis uses charts to identify significant market trends or specific stock turns. The use of technical analysis, like fundamental analysis, is to help reduce risk.

Technical analysis' most useful function is to help confirm a movement that seems unrealistic, too hopeful, or even unpopular. Charts tell us things like a doctor does — what is the past history, the diagnosis, the chances, the effect of certain factors like diet or exercise.

This section is about fundamental analysis. I read the technical books, and study their methods, and I use what I understand, but pure numbers have never had that much appeal to me. I like the challenge of figuring out movements, values—entrance and exit points. While I love technical information, I also love the basics, the fundamentals. I use both, but ultimately base my decisions on my own "gut feeling" after looking at all the data I can collect.

The main reason I favor the fundamental approach is that all movements have their genesis in one or more of the fundamental aspects of the stock. Fundamental approaches take a "separate" or a dispassionate look at the stock (or the market). Technical aspects of movements are not apart from, but integral to the stock or the market movements. Fundamentals give people opinions, while technicals try to confirm those opinions.

Whichever method you favor, trying to predict the future movement is the goal, and trying to reduce risk along the way in order to forecast these movements is what separates winners from losers. Yes, there is risk, but you know you can't get something for nothing. Risk is the price you pay for the rewards.

The following fundamentals are the five main methods or tools to help you make good decisions, to hit a lot of singles and a few homers, all the while trying to avoid too many strike outs.

1) EARNINGS

We will first discuss earnings and earnings per share, or P/E. The earnings of a company are its bottom line—they are the profits (after taking out dividends to shareholders of any preferred stock and after taxes).

To figure the earnings per share, we take the number of shares outstanding and divide it into earnings—hence we get earnings per share. *Earnings are very important* and are that which the company uses for dividend payouts, for investment in growth, for excess debt reduction. This figure is most often used by lending institutions for calculation of new debt paybacks.

Earnings should be from sales, and not from one time phenomenons like the sale of a division, or a bad investment charge off. Many sources list earnings per share: *Barron's, Investor's Business Daily*, most local newspapers with financial information, and most computer on-line services.

In determining your stock purchases, you'll not only want current figures but you'll want to know where the company has been. Does it have a history of increasing earnings? Did they increase, then slow down? You need to understand why the earnings per share are what they are.

The P/E is a very important number. I teach this from coast to coast. "When in doubt," I say, "follow earnings." Yes, the other measuring sticks are useful but not as important as earnings. Think of it. Some companies just don't need a lot of assets to produce income. Some need a lot of assets and other forms of overhead.

The P/E is stated in terms that let us figure how much each dollar of stock is making. If the company's stock is trading at $80 and it earns $8 per share, it has a multiple of 10. If it's making $4 per share, it has a multiple, or P/E of 20; 20 times $4 equals $80. Another way would be to divide the $4 into $80 and get 20, or P/E 20. In this case, what we're saying as investors is that we are willing to accept a 5% cash flow return (even though we may not actually receive the $4 or the $8); 5% of $80 is $4.

As I've said, P/E's are very, very important. We need to understand how to use them—and how to keep them in perspective.

To decide if a P/E for a particular company is good, we need to: 1) Pick a number we're happy with—say, "I'll buy any company with a P/E under 14," or 2) compare it to the market as a whole, or 3) compare it to stocks in the same sector, say high-tech or pharmaceuticals.

Let's look at #2, as #1 is self-explanatory. *Standard and Poors* has a stock index of 500 stocks. It's called the S&P 500. The combined P/E for these companies is in the mid-teens. Lately, it's moved to the mid- or upper-teens. You compare your company to this number and get a feel for how well it's doing.

You could also look at a smaller picture and compare your stock to other companies in the same business. There are so many variables in trying to get a handle on this information. One problem is that different reporting services use different time periods. For example, one newspaper may use "trailing 12 months" numbers to figure a company's P/E. It could be accurate to the last decimal, but is it appropriate to make a judgment solely based on where a company has been? Are we not buying the future—what a company <u>will</u> earn? Some figures are on projected earnings. Well, if we only used this number, would that be complete—as if anybody knows what a company will actually earn? Yes, analysts (for the company or independent) can make their best guess, but they often fall short or overstate earnings.

Probably the best gauge would be to take a blend of the "trailing" and the "projected earnings." Many papers report it in some combination: say, trailing 12 and future 12 months. Many use 6 months back and 6 months future.

A couple of thoughts:

1) I have been such an adamant proponent of caution in buying stocks. So many investors get caught up in the hype of it all. Yes, I agree we all have to recognize the sensational and buy into it a little—but very little. "Follow earnings, follow earnings," I shout. People who have attended my seminars and even some of my employees have drowned me out. Let me give an example by way of a story.

Iomega (IOM) is a high tech, software company. The stock got to new highs and kept going up. They announced a stock split (I really like stock splits) and the stock soared. I got in at $14 and $16 and sold out at $30—a really nice profit. The stock went to $50. The hype was still in the air. I bought some $40 options, even though I knew the stock was way overpriced. I got out in days with a double on some and triple on others. The stock went over $60 and headed for $80.

Everyone was getting in—in both stock and options. I stopped. These numbers put the P/E over 100. I think it hit 120 times earnings at one time.

At my seminars, in my office, and on W.I.N. (our computer bulletin board service) I shouted: "I am not playing," "the bubble has got to burst," and "it's way too high." Yes, I might miss out, but this high price can't be sustained. Also, I had been following Iomega for some time as a nice, little, volatile, covered call play, and this time around I wasn't going for it. This all happened between the spring of 1996 and the fall of the same year.

It's hard to buy a stock at $50 when you were buying it for $14 just months before. Yes, it's earnings were up a little, but not that much. The price was not justified.

It did another split. It was a 2:1. The stock split down to the $30 range and went back up to $40. This is when it was at 120 times earnings.

I held no positions, but everyone around me did no matter how hard I tried to stop them. I calculated the stocks (based on earnings and a little hype thrown in) ought to be around $23 per share. I was throwing in about $10 per share for the "internet hype" value. It was really a $12 to $15 stock.

This next part will seem like a joke but it's true. When the stock was way up there, analysts for the company were trying to justify the high price. They actually made comments like: "The price isn't so high based on projected earnings three years from now." That's right. Three years. Talk about hype. But tens of thousands of people bought into it.

Guess what? It fell to $30, then to $24—almost overnight it was at $16. Then it trickled on down to $13. It rebounded to 13½ to 14½ and I started jumping back in. I bought stock, options, and sold puts. I loaded up. I sold out within weeks, before and when it hit $27.

I'll play it a lot, but not when the price is too high. One of the questions you must ask is this: What must the company do to sustain this price? The hype-sters that run up a stock are gone; and it could take years to recover from buying too high. Be careful! Follow earnings!

2) The market is crazy, and if not totally wacky, at least hard to understand. This example has played out recently in scenario after scenario. Here's a typical example: A stock is at $60. An analyst (someone with: What kind of education? What kind of real-world experience in running companies? What kind of motivation?) projects that in the next year the company will earn $3 per share. He/she calculated this by taking numbers supplied by the company, etc., etc. and putting the numbers through some kind of filter—possibly what other companies in the same field are saying or are doing, and comes up with the $3. This is a P/E of 20 and not bad for this sector. (See P/E for NYSE and NASDAQ). He/she recommends the stock as a buy. Not a strong buy, just a buy, and thousands of investors and funds start to buy. The stock goes up to $62 on this recommendation but within weeks it's back down to $60.

Let's thicken the plot a little. More information. Last year the company earnings were $2.90 per share. For this type of business this is a nice profit. The year before it was at $2.40 per share and the year before that it was $1.50 per share. It's had a nice increase.

Time passes and the actual earnings are $2.97 per share. The analyst was off 3¢ and the stock falls to $52, dropping $8 off its value. You think I'm joking, but I can show you a long list of this same story played out repeatedly.

The company is profitable, it's growing, it's earning millions—more than the previous year—but alas, the stock gets killed. Note: This author looks for these opportunities. See other sections for taking advantage of these serious dips.

More thoughts on P/E:

- To make sure you're not overpaying for a stock, watch the P/E in changing markets. In a Bull market the P/E can be higher. In a Bear market you would expect a lower P/E.

- Certain industries have different P/E's. Banks have low P/E's—say, in the 5 to 12 range. High tech companies have higher P/E's—say, around 15 to 30. Check the sector to see what you're paying.

- If your bank P/E is at 9 and the average is 8, you are paying a premium for the stock. It's okay if you expect higher earnings. If your food sector P/E is 16 and the company you're considering has a P/E of 12, then you're getting it at a discount.

- A low P/E is not a pure indication of value. You need to consider its price volatility (See "Beta"), its range, its direction, and any news you think worthy.

- You may want to check the historical level (P/E) of the stock. If the current P/E is above the 5 or 15 year historical P/E, the movement of the stock may be about to drop back into line.

IMPORTANT: The activities or news of a company—that which has driven the P/E to its current level—does you no good prior to your stock purchase. This is why you also need to look at, consider, and take into account the future earnings estimates. Yes, be careful, but remember, you make your money after you buy the stock so it is the future that will pay you—in dividends and in growth.

2) YIELDS

A company may take some of the cash it has available and pay it out to the shareholders of record. This is called a dividend. It is done on a per share basis. By dividing the amount by the price of each share, you would find the yield or rate of return.

Example: A stock is at $30 and $2 (annual equivalent) is to be paid—that would be a 6.66% return.

Using the dividend yield to determine whether to buy a stock or not is informative, but by no means complete. In the opening sentence I mentioned cash available. I did not say profits or earnings. The dividend could be paid out of debt.

Imagine this: A company has paid dividends every quarter for 13 years, and every payout is slightly larger than the previous quarter. You think all is well. But lately market share of the company's products are slipping. The directors meet. They've seen their stock value continually rise. They feel the shareholders need to see the dividend and see it in an ever-increasing amount. But their cash flow has dried up. They borrow money for operations and to pay the dividends. They also feel, at first, that they can turn things around.

The dividend is paid like this for five quarters as the company slips toward complete insolvency and possible bankruptcy. Eventually the dividend stops and the stock plummets.

Point: Dividend yield is important but you need to:

1) Keep it in perspective

2) Seek other information

   - read the company's balance sheets

   - get reports from information sources

3) Do not rely solely on yields for justification for buying or selling a stock.

Good Earnings—Low Yield

Let's go to the other extreme. A company is doing well. Debt is decreasing, earnings are up and increasing, but the dividend payout is rather small, say 2.1%. What gives? Yes, they can pay out more, but the choice is made not to. Corporate directors, in the past 20 years—in our new information society—have had to become experts in many fields. One is taxation.

In the current tax code, dividends are not deductible. The company has to pay taxes on all dividends. The corporation may be in the 15%, 25%, 31%, or 35% tax bracket. When you, the shareholder, receive the dividend, you also have to claim and pay taxes on it—and do so in whatever bracket you are in. This seriously reduces your rate of return. This is double taxation. It's sad that we have politicians who treat us so callously.

Think of this. The company has a $10,000,000 profit. They pay $3,500,000 in taxes. For the sake of this argument, let's say it was all to be paid out in dividends. Your check is $2,000, and you are in the 31% tax bracket. That's an additional $620 to go to the IRS. Yes, the IRS gets 66% in this example. It's a staggering amount. I'd like to comment on the ghastly things they do with this huge amount of money, but I'll restrain myself.

Now imagine a meeting of the directors. If they pay out the money (hopefully from true earnings) to you, they know you will be taxed. The corporation will get taxed no matter what, but they can stop the second level of taxation by simply not paying it. Also, if they could take this money and expand the business, pay down debt—in other words, increase the value of the company—would you not be better off?

Remember our earnings multipliers. Let's say the company has a P/E of 15 but it takes this money, using it wisely, and generates 30% more profits. The earnings go way up. Will not the stock value increase? And think, until we sell the stock and have capital gains taxes to pay, the growth is tax free. We could own stock for years with no tax consequences.

Simply put. We want the directors to do the best job they can. If we are investing solely for income (and will take the growth as a bonus) then we may want to find stocks with nice dividend payouts. But most of us should look for companies with great earnings, and hope this money is used effectively to build more value into the stocks we own.

3) BOOK VALUE

When purchasing stock, one has to ask the question: what is it really worth? In the real estate arena the cliche answer is: whatever someone is willing to pay for it.

It is not quite that simple in picking stocks. One measurement of equity is called the book value. It is the dollar amount you get when you subtract all the liabilities (including preferred stock) from the assets. This figure then could be divided by the number of shares outstanding and get the value per share. With this number in hand, we can see: 1) how much of each share is real value—possibly expressed as breakup value; 2) we can see how the book value of the company compares with other companies; and subsequently; 3) this value can be used to figure other percentages—as in sales to book: an assessment to determine the percentage of sales to the book value of the company.

Again, the main reason we study this is to make sure we are not overpaying for the stock. I am willing to buy into the excitement of a stock but when the price gets outrageous, even above that which is justified by earnings and way over book value, then it becomes a little scary.

In theory, you would want what the stock is trading at to be the same as the book value. The book value is $30 per share and the stock is $30 per share. But in reality, all stocks trade at a premium (the share price is above the book value/per share amount) or at a discount (the share price is below the book value per share amount).

Most stocks trade at a premium. I'm constantly on the lookout for companies trading below book value. All else being equal, you're getting the stock wholesale. I really frown on stocks at over 3 times book value. If the earnings justify the higher price, I might go for it. But I like stock trading at $1^1/_2$ to 2 times the book value. If you are after stocks which trade even, you'll have to look a long time and possibly end up buying nothing.

Don't despair when you see a great company at $2^1/_2$ to $3^1/_2$ times book value. Consider the following: A company has purchased real estate—buildings & factories. They also own a lot of equipment. These are all depreciable items for tax purposes.

According to GAAP (Generally Accepted Accounting Principles) it must carry on its books the value of these assets at **cost** or **market,** whichever is <u>LESS</u>. This adds an unrealistic dimension to the calculation of book value.

An example is in order. XYZ company purchases a $10,000,000 factory. It depreciates it over the years to $6,000,000, but in fact the building is actually worth $14,000,000. The amount on the company books (as an asset) is $6,000,000. The same with trucks, computers, and other equipment. And these depreciate faster. You see by this how difficult it is to get a proper "fix" on what a company is really worth.

To protect yourself:

1) Go out and "kick the tires"—really check the company out. Do your homework.

2) Learn how to get "behind the scenes" financial infor mation.

3) Use book value in conjunction with other measuring devices.

Not all low book value companies are bad deals. Usually a low book value means there is not a large belief that a stock price will increase. Maybe it's in an unfavorable industry. There are many good companies with low book values. Also, there are companies ready to explode which have a current high book value ratio.

One possible play is to look for companies with low book value because they are often the target of a takeover. Other companies want to get at their assets and can buy at bargain rates if the stock is trading at or below book value, or if the book value figure does not properly represent true book value.

Book value is extremely important. Look for companies with a low book value percentage, but keep everything in perspective. Book value is also referred to as "Shareholder Equity." What kind of income and growth do you want your equity to produce?

4) EQUITY RETURNS

I hinted at this in the last section on Book Value. We want our equity to be producing for us. In real estate, it's how much income it can produce. Department stores measure part of their success by "sales per square foot." What are our assets making?

Return on stock equity is the company's after tax profits divided by the book value. The important thing here is to see if this return is increasing from year to year. These numbers are usually found in the company's annual report.

5) DEBT RATIO

I've saved the best 'till last. Actually, this is not the most important measurement of stock value—that realm is reserved for earnings, but this runs a close second place.

This ratio shows the percentage of debt a company has in relationship to shareholder equity. You want this to be low. The actual figure varies from company to company. Just remember debt is a killer of businesses. Yes, the company may have a well marketed product; yes, cash flow is up, but it may not be enough to cover the debt load.

Let's say a company has shareholder equity of $100,000,000. Debt is $30,000,000. This is a ratio of 30%. Some companies have debt as high at 70% to 90%. That is way too high, because the earnings are decreased so much to service the debt.

This author (again, many other variables enter the picture) wants the debt to be under 30%. I usually shy away from 50% or higher debt ratios.

There are several other smaller measurement techniques, and all are helpful to a certain extent. The "Big 5" just mentioned should be in your toolbox to help you make intelligent and timely decisions.

No one measurement alone is foolproof, and even when all five point to a recommended buy, the whole market may turn down.

Remember, these tools are to help you take the best calculated risk possible. When in doubt, remember my strongest advice from my seminars: "Follow earnings."

6

OPTIMUM OPTIONS

AN INTRODUCTION TO PROXY INVESTING

More bang for the buck! That's what we all want. Wise use of stock options is one way to get it. This chapter is about using a form of proxy investing to leverage greater returns. And returns, to me, mean extra income, not just an increase in value.

Throughout all my real estate books and courses and now in my stock market educational materials, I stress "cash-flow" concepts and techniques. After all, is it not cash flow that pays the bills and lets us get into an ever-increasing upward spiral of income?

Buying or selling options to purchase stock are simple strategies loaded with opportunities. There are variations on purchase and exit strategies, and combination plays both with the underlying stock and with other options. Options are derivatives of an investment on an underlying security. A call option is the right to buy a stock at a fixed strike price anytime before a set date. A put option is similar, but is the right to sell. Both calls and puts expire. They end. This expiration is one inherent risk of option investing.

Why would anyone want such a risk? Simply because of the fantastic profits which can be made in a very short period of time. You see, an option moves up and down in value with the movement of the stock, but to be precise, it moves on an exaggerated scale. I'll explain this as I go along and illustrate it with examples. Once we're through with the basics (and I refer you to the book, *The Wall Street Money Machine* for more details) I'll show you a few, heavy-duty strategies to get you making more money.

Example: You could buy a stock for $86. The stock seems down right now; you think it will go back up to $92 or $96, where it's been trading for some time. It's March. You check the May $90 call options (the right to buy the stock at $90 per share before the May expiration date). The call options are $2.50 each. You'll spend $250 plus commission for one contract (a contract contains 100 shares of stock). $2,500 would purchase 10 contracts. You could also buy the $85 calls, the $95 calls or other strike prices, and you might be better served by buying options with a different expiration month than May. (I explore short-term and long-term plays in my other special reports and in other chapters.)

Your $2.50 option premium gives you the right to buy the stock at $90. Obviously you want the stock to rise. Many people suggest the stock would have to go to $92.50 for you to break even and above that for any profit. A better understanding of the strategy, though, will help you see that the stock doesn't have to rise that high for us to be profitable.

Options are bought and sold like stocks. There is a trader (like a market maker or specialist) who buys and sells. Like stock, you don't know who purchases your option—it just happens. Options have bids and asks. A bid is what you can sell it for, the ask is the price you pay to buy. The bid and the ask move up and down according to several factors: 1) the supply and demand for the option, 2) the time left before the expiration date, and 3) other market sentiments. For example, with tremendously erratic stock, the market makers keep a high option premium because they know the stock has the potential to make big swings. Also note: you do not have to trade at the current bid and ask. You can place orders to buy below the ask or an order to sell above the bid. These orders can be day orders only or "good till cancelled" (GTC) orders. It costs nothing to place the order.

Watch the movement of the option compared with the stock price in the following example. Look at the $88 price. The option is $3.75. This will not stay constant. This $88/$3.75 quote is, say, six weeks before the expiration date. If it were six days, the option could be $1.25. You see, an option buys time. A part of the premium is the time value. In our example, the $3.75 is all time value. Why did it go down to $1.25? Because "the invisible market" doesn't believe very strongly that in six days the stock will go up to or above $90. If the stock stays at $88, the option probably will expire worthless. However, look at what happens when the stock goes above $90. The option has become more valuable. Someone is willing to pay $4.75 for the

Stock/Strike	Stock Price	Option (Call)
	$84	$1.00
XYZ Company	85	2.00
May $90 Call option	86	2.46
	87	3.00
	88	3.75
(Note: The premium	90	4.75
depends on time before	91	5.50
expiration—see note.)	92	6.50

right to buy the stock at $90. If the stock goes to $98, the option could be worth $8 to $9 (or more), again depending on the time left before expiration.

If the stock is $92 and the option is $6.50, you see that $2 of the $6.50 is actually paying for stock. The option is "in the money" by $2 (intrinsic value). $4.50 of the option premium is time value (extrinsic value).

Now, the main question: What is our purpose in buying the option? Do we want to buy the stock? Maybe, but this author is waiting for the options to gain value so they can be sold at a profit. If we purchased the options for $2.50 and can now sell it for $4.50 (assuming the bid and ask is something like $4.50 x $4.75), we have a $2 profit. If we had purchased ten contracts, that would be $2,000.

Let's review the word "exaggerated." In this example a $1 movement in the stock means a 50¢ movement in the option. Sometimes the stock to option movement ratio could be "tick for tick," or dollar for dollar. A dollar rise in the stock produces a dollar rise in the option. The point is you have much less cash tied up. $2,500 controls 1,000 shares of stock. You didn't invest $86,000 buying 1,000 shares of stock. Also, a $1 move in the stock from $86 to $87 is around a 1% gain. If this creates a 50¢ move in the option from $2.50 to $3, it is a 20% gain.

If you sell the $2.50 option for $4.50, the $4,500 cash will be in your account tomorrow. Options clear in one day.

After attending the first day of your workshop, I was confident that with some diligence one could in fact use the techniques you taught. The second day in class, with increased confidence, I made my first two rolling option purchases during the morning's "early bird" session.

To my pleasant surprise, I was able to sell both options the following morning for a profit large enough to cover the complete cost of the workshop. I have contributed around $31,125 in the last 15 days, and thus have been able to clear a net profit of $23,252.35 after commissions. Yes, that's right, 74.7% in 15 days and an annual percentage rate of 1,817%.

I'm still pinching myself to see if I'm awake! I am now eagerly waiting to attend The Next S.T.E.P. Wall Street Workshop and hold even greater expectations in mind.

Michael—Kent, Washington

Yes, we've all seen stock go up $2 to $10 in, or within, a day. Think about buying an option an hour after the market opens for 50¢ and selling it for $1.50 two hours later. Ten contracts would generate a $1,000 profit.

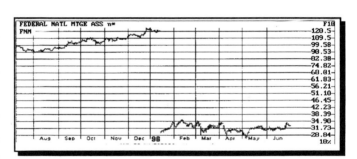

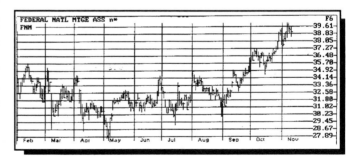

Let's do the same on a put. Last year, Fannie Mae (FNM) did a 4 for 1 stock split. A few months later, the stock was rolling between $31.50 and $36. News came out that the long bond yield was down 3 points. This is the U.S. Treasury 30-year bond. The stock market was hammered that day. There were other things going on also. Fannie Mae is very interest-rate sensitive, as they borrow money at one rate and lend it out at another, higher rate. If the interest rates go up (that's why the long bond was falling—fear of inflation and a rise in rates), the stock can really go down. Likewise, if interest rates go down, the stock might go up.

To put it mildly, the stock got slammed. I knew it would go down. I put it on the Wealth Information Network (W.I.N.) immediately, telling my students how I was going to play it. The stock closed Friday at about $33. It opened at $31.75 (on a 30-minute delayed opening). I purchased the March $32.50 puts.

This lets me "put" the stock to someone else at $32.50. If the stock goes under $32.50, my put option becomes more valuable. It's the opposite of a call. As the stock goes down, the put becomes worth more. I bought these puts for $1^1/$_8$ or $1.125. The stock went down to $27^1/$_2$ and as it bounced back up to $29 to $30, I sold the put for $3^5/$_8$. That's a four-hour play and a nice profit of $2,500. $3,625 minus $1,125=$2,500 (minus commissions of about $110 for both trades).

If you buy options, you do not have the obligation to buy or sell the stock. You also don't have to sell the option—you could just let it expire. You have the "right" to buy or sell. Again, though, I don't buy the options to buy the stock. I buy options hoping for an increase in value and then sell them. It's just quick-turn money.

I have a "bear market mentality" in the midst of a bull market. I really don't like losing money. Options are very risky—only 15% to 20% of contracts ever get exercised. That's not to say there are many losses, as some investors like me get in and get out rapidly. I have lost on several plays, and each time I do, I vow to never do that again. I want to learn from my mistakes; I've cut the losses to a bare minimum. I'm now somewhere in the range of one loser for every 18 to 20 winners. You can watch me do this on W.I.N., Wade Cook Seminar's computer bulletin board service.

> *Here is how my trades have gone since I started using W.I.N. I bought two Xerox (XRX) $125 April call options for $6.75 and sold them one week later for $10.75, a profit of $663 (49.1%). I also bought two Warner Lambert (WLA) $90 April call options for $6.75 and just sold them nine days later for $10.25, a profit of $562 (41.6%).*
>
> *I'm shooting for 50% returns on covered call writing, all profits to be reinvested until I'm consistently pulling enough per month to be able to retire and do what I want with my life. Now there's hope and light at the end of the tunnel. All my thanks go to Wade and everybody there on the W.I.N. staff.*
>
> *Augustin*

You'll see my "hunker down," try-not-to-lose-a-penny strategies permeating the following formulas.

BUY ON DIPS

One of my longtime favorite ways to make money on options is to buy when the stock takes a serious dip. Check the company's story though, to avoid further downturns. Look at the following charts:

Motorola (MOT): The stock was $70 to $80 a share. It's a great company. Earnings were up but not what analysts expected (the whole high-tech arena was down) and the stock plunged to the low $50 range. I purchased the $55 calls and some $60 calls. When the stock rose, I sold the calls at a nice profit. I'm always doing this play with a dozen or so companies.

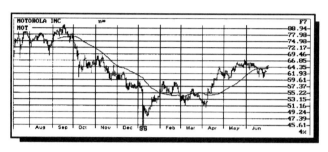

I like Organogenesis (ORG). When it dipped down to $19, I jumped back in. I'm doing both a pure option play and a covered call play. There are so many companies which fall into this category.

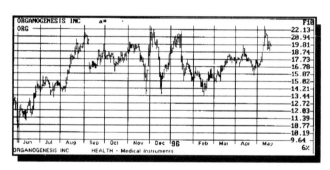

Rolling Options

After a company takes a big dip, the climb back up is volatile. Sometimes it stays down for a while and starts trading between a certain range. I call this rolling stock. If you follow my formula for a pure rolling stock play as outlined in the *Wall Street Money Machine* and at our live Wall Street

Workshop, you'll realize that $50 to $100 stocks don't fit the formula. They're priced too high. Your cash goes a short distance with an $80 stock. $8,000 buys 100 shares. Yes, a move to $85 would make you $500, but a $5 move on a $5 stock would also make you $500, but with only $500 tied up. A better example: $8,000 would purchase 1,600 shares of a $5 stock. A $5 move up would double your money. Upon selling you'd have $16,000—a profit of $8,000. Now to make it more exciting and still double your money (because there are many more companies at $80 which can easily go to $85 than there are companies at $5 which go to $10), let's play an option.

The stock is at $80. You call your broker and buy the $85 call options, say two months out. You pay $1.25 per option and buy ten contracts for $1,250. The stock moves up to $84. Your option is worth $3.75. You sell for a $2.50 profit and make $2,500. Look at the power of leverage.

Options allow you to invest in the big stocks by proxy, using a small amount of money.

Look back at the chart on Motorola (page 90). Every time the stock goes down to $50-$52, I buy the $55 call option. I'm not hoping the stock goes back up to $100, though it would be nice, and I'm not doing this to buy the stock. I'm simply going to sell my $1.25 option for $2.50 or $3.50 when the stock rolls up. Another day, another week, another $10,000 profit.

Some stocks just seem to trade in a certain range (support at the bottom, resistance at the top.) Check out Ford (F). It rolls be-

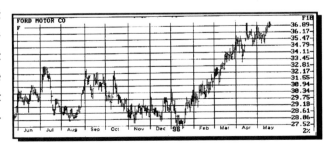

tween $27 and $34. When it gets down to $27 or $28, I buy the $30 calls or the $35 calls if they are cheap. I sell them when the stock gets to $32-$33. Don't get greedy. Get out, get your profits working better somewhere else. If it gets to $34 or $35, I then buy the $35 puts. As it falls back to $30 or under, I sell them. This past year, this has been a bankable play.

Wade Cook's workshop . . . was a skeptical seminar for me to go to, even though I have invested in the stock market for several years. My first attempt at options was at the WSWS last week. I generated $3,256 in one day's time while at the workshop! Since then, in the next week, I made another $2,270. I am excited about the opportunity to be home with my children while I am making money for my husband's and my retirement. Thank you for teaching me a few formulas and hands-on experience.

Dawn—Poway, California

SELLING STRADDLES

By definition, a straddle is writing (selling) a call option and a put option on the same stock with the same strike price and expiration date. In the sameness is the simplicity. The same stock. The same number of contracts (call and put). The same strike price. The same expiration date. Notice that I am selling both a call and a put, which generates money into my account from both sales. Though it is not exactly doubling my cash in, it does come close to doing that.

There are some potentially expensive risks, however. This is not a strategy for everyone. If the stock suddenly makes a big move in either direction, I could be caught. Remember, I haven't bought any stock and I have sold someone the right to force me to sell the stock to or buy stock from them.

If the stock goes up and I get called out, I will have to buy the stock (in order to sell it). Since the stock went up, the person who sold the put option (who was betting that the stock would go down) is not likely to exercise his or her option. This is because he or she can sell their stock for more on the open market than they could force me to buy it for. The put option will expire.

If the stock goes down or stays under the strike price, I don't have to worry about being called out because the person who bought the call option from me can buy the stock on the open market for less than they would have to pay if they exercised the option and bought the stock directly from me. The person who sold the put, however, can force me to buy his/her stock for the option price.

This is not a loss. I am simply paying more for the stock than I might have. What I get when I sell the stock will determine whether I have a gain or loss. The money I received from selling the options will offset the difference between what I paid and what I sold the stock for.

Before I write a straddle, I spend a lot of time with my broker evaluating what the cash flow will be and what the risk of loss could be. I won't typically write a straddle unless the risk potential and the cash flow is substantial. You'll need to make your own decisions in this area. Most of the time, the stock stays close to the strike price and both options expire leaving me with all the money. Occasionally, one of the options will be exercised and I'll have to give back some of the premium I received from selling the options, but I get to keep most of it.

HEDGE A STOCK

One last use for options is a "hedge." A hedge is like an insurance policy. You hedge to limit your downside.

Let's say you just spent $10,000 and purchased 100 shares of stock at $100 each. You think the stock is low (either the company is really profitable or that the stock has gone down – hit a low). That's a lot of money to have tied up. You have unlimited upside potential and all the time in the world because you actually own the stock. Your only risk is a dip in the price of the stock.

To ensure against a loss in your stock value, buy a $100 put, or even a $95 put (if you are willing to lose a little). Yes, you could put in a stop loss, at, say, $97 and only lose $300, but what about a drop to $70 wherein you could lose $3,000. The $100 put is, say, $2. One contract (controlling 100 shares—the same amount you own) would cost $200 plus commission. If you never exercise the put, that's $200 out the window. You bought the stock hoping it would go up, and if it does your $200 ($2 put) goes down in value. Any increase in the value of your $10,000 investment will be offset by this loss. However, if the stock goes down, and I mean seriously down, this $200 will be money well spent. If the stock goes down to $80 (assuming this is still before the expiration date of the put) your put will be worth at least $20. It could be $22 to $25 depending on any time value still built into the put premium.

Think of this. You could sell the stock for $80 and also sell the put premium for $20. That's $8,000 and $2,000 respectively. You've broken even. You see the insurance-against-loss aspect of this. You could lose $200 or at least have your profits offset by this amount, but you can make up all your losses with the proper put.

Two more ideas: The $95 put might be purchased for 25¢ when the stock is at $100. One contract would be $25 plus commissions. This lower strike price and the corresponding lower put premium will let you buy a put further out (say 5 to 6 months) for a lower price. Your risk is $500 plus the put premium. Why $500? Because you've lost the amount between $100 for the stock and $95. 100 shares times $5 equals $500.

The $100 put is $2 and it's only out one to two months. I usually buy the short-term puts at the higher strike price (out one to two months and then reevaluate the situation: company news, the stock price near the expiration date, etc.) or further out puts below the strike price. They're cheaper but also give you more time.

By looking at the company's chart you can determine how much you want to spend, how much time you want to buy, and how much risk you want to hedge.

COMBO

You could also buy a call with a $100 or $110 strike price. If you're certain this stock is a winner, go ahead and buy the stock for $10,000, but spend $500 and purchase the $105 calls out two to three months. If the stock rises, you'll see first hand how the riskier option plays produce the greater returns.

7

The Put-ting Green

This chapter was written to dispel the mystery of "put" options and give several serious strategies for generating cash flow from either buying or selling puts.

A put option, as opposed to a call option, gives an investor the right to sell a stock. We will be concerned with stock options only in this chapter. A put option could be defined in street jargon as the right to "put it to someone." You would want to put a stock to someone when you can purchase the stock at a lower price and sell it (immediately) at a higher price. For example, if you notice a stock consistently climbing above $30 to $33 or $35, and it not only has a hard time getting to the higher level, but also has a hard time sustaining the higher price, then you may want to buy a $35 put. As the stock comes back down, your "right" to sell the stock for $35 increases in value. As with call options, I do not buy the option to sell the stock. I buy the option to sell the option.

More About Selling Options

Options are fickle. They don't always mirror the exact stock movement. A lot of things enter the picture:

1) The volatility of the stock. What does the options market know? Sometimes, it seems they know more than the stock market.

2) The time remaining before the option expires. After all, when buying an option, you are paying for two things: time (extrinsic value), and part of the price of the stock (intrinsic value) if you are purchasing an "in the money" option.

If you purchase a $2 call option on a $35 strike price when the stock is at $33, and the stock moves to $36, your option could easily be worth $4 to $6, depending on the time left before the expiration date. However, if the stock goes no-where, and then rises to $36 with ten days to go before the expiration date, it may only be worth the same $2. If the stock halts at $36 and the time elapses to the point that there is only a day or so left, the option may trade for just the one dollar and the option is in the money. In this example, a $36 stock with a $35 strike price is $1 in the money. When investing in options, time is both our friend and our enemy. The value of the option has a direct and distinct relationship to the expi-ration date. All other factors: price, volatile movement, and market maker maneuvering, aid and abet the "fixed time" aspect of the option value. Hence, options can be extremely profitable, yet very risky.

Stock options are sold in 100 share increments. When you purchase one contract, you are actually purchasing the right to buy or sell 100 shares. Strike prices are the same for calls and puts. Stocks priced in the $5 to $25 range are sold in $2.50 increments. Stocks priced in the $25 to $200 range are sold in $5 increments, and stocks priced above $200 are sold in $10 increments. Note: as the options market becomes more popular, there are more strike prices added. For example, if a stock has a high trading volume, the option "market maker" may add an additional strike price, such as $32.50 or $57.50.

THE "PUT" OPTION

Stock options are different from other options in that you actually control the right to buy or sell the underlying security.

Let's keep exploring the "put" option. Keep in mind, if you are following the Wade Cook formula, you are not purchasing the option to purchase the stock, but to have inventory to sell as the option increases in value. Look at the following chart and you'll see an increasing put value.

Stock	Strike	Put Option
34	35	$2.00
33	35	$2.50
32	35	$3.25
31	35	$4.50
30	35	$5.75
29	35	$7.00
28	35	$8.00

Example: It's October and we purchased the January $35 puts.

Your put option increases in value as the stock moves away from the strike price. If the stock is $31 and the strike price is $35, the value of your option has to be at least $4. Indeed, you could buy the stock at $31 and sell it to someone for $35. This put option gives you that right.

Options expire on the third Friday of the month, but you may exercise your option at any time on or before the expiration date. Or, you may sell your option anytime there is an open bid. Options have a bid and an ask like stocks. You can sell at any price you choose, and one of those choices may be a market order (which is also known as the current bid).

The sentence which brings options to life and the one I repeat in all my seminars holds true for put options as well. Here it is:

> **When there is a small movement in the stock, there is a magnified movement in the option.**

Revisit the previous diagram. A move of $3 in stock price, about 10% down in the stock, took the option from $2.50 to $4.50, a huge percentage move. With a call option you don't need to double the price of the stock to double your money on the option, and with put options you don't need a stock to drop half of its value to double your put option value. Frequently, small stock movements equal large option movements.

When the options start moving, you have several choices.

1) Sell it for a price you're happy with.

    A) This could be done by placing a sell order anytime after you own the option, even immediately— usually at a higher price.

    B) You can wait and watch the stocks, trying to plan your exit to maximize your profits.

Which one do you choose? In my case it usually depends on how busy I am. If I have a lot of plays going on, or if my other business endeavors take up my time, I usually place the sell order when I make my purchase. I place it high enough to get a nice large profit. If the option doesn't move that high, I move the price down or just go ahead and sell. Note: pay attention as the expiration date nears.

2) Exercise the underlying stock (buy or sell), but again, this is not why I play options.

3) Sell part of your position, five contracts out of the ten. Ride the five you keep to greater profits. It's possible to get a free ride, in that the profits from the five contracts you sold could "get back" all or most of your investment. Now, you have nothing to lose.

Before I get into specific strategies, let me remind you of the underlying current of my trades—it is to make millions by executing minor trades, even on the same stock, at different strike prices and expiration months. Why?

1) I don't have a lot of cash tied up in any one deal.

2) I can take advantage of frequent, small swings and not wait for rare, "killer" moves.

3) I like the cash flow. There are always other deals. Take all or some of your profits and jump back in if the stock moves back up, choosing a different strike price. If you sold your $35 strike price and more bad news came out, maybe a purchase of the $30 strike price would be in order. If the stock has dipped way down and you're highly profitable, take some of your money and:

A) Buy some of the stock—hoping for a rebound.

B) Buy call options and ride the stock back up.

C) Generate more cash flow by selling puts (see the section on selling puts).

There are three put formulas which you can use for generating income. I hope you'll note that inherent to these formulas are the "risk eliminators," which, hopefully, will keep us out of trouble.

FORMULA #1—ROLLING OPTIONS

The development of this formula has its genesis in my rolling stock strategy. Play options on stocks trading within a specific range. I like the less expensive stocks because it doesn't take too much movement to make a great profit. However, most stocks that are doing nice, steady rolls between a high and a low are in higher dollar amounts, say between $27 and $33, or $98 and $104. It would take a lot of cash to buy them, and there just may be better uses of our money. If the roll continues, there is definitely a better way to play the roll: proxy investing. Do options on stocks that trade within a certain range.

The strategy is simple: buy call options when the stock is low and wait for the roll up. Next, sell the call option and then buy put options when the stock peaks. Take your profits when it rolls back down. I've written about this concept elsewhere so I won't belabor the call play here. Let's explore the put strategy.

Volatility and predictability and using the extra cash you can afford to lose, bring a higher degree of certainty to this risky arena. This is a tremendous formula in which you can get to be an expert.

FORMULA #2—PUT VARIATIONS

This formula requires volatility, but we also like predictability. I'll encourage you once again to subscribe to a charting service. (I use *Telechart 2000*® by Worden Brothers. Wade Cook Seminars has a start-up kit for sale. Call 1-800-872-7411. It's inexpensive, but invaluable.)

To begin, you track a stock. Let's say it continues to peak (hits resistance) every time it gets to $35. Obviously it could break out at any point and go to a new high, so make sure you can stand the risk, but for the past while it hasn't gone above $35.

For quite a few months $35 has been the high. Buy the $35 put, or if you think

Stock Price	$30 put	$35 put	$40 put
$34.75	$1.50	$3.00	$6.75
34.00	1.25	3.375	7.25
33.00	1.75	4.00	8.125
32.00	2.50	4.75	9.00
30.00	4.00	6.50	10.50
28.00	6.00	7.875	12.50
27.00	6.75	8.75	13.50

the stock is going to go way down, play the $30 put. Let's say the stock is at $34³/₄. The $35 put is $3. That's a fairly high premium. Very little of the option premium is in the money with this put. "In the money" means the stock is below the strike price. In this case, just 25¢ is in the money. We check the $30 puts and they're going for 75¢. They're cheap because the stock, at this strike price, is so far out of the money. The stock has to take a big move downward for you to get to the $30 strike price. Now remember, the stock doesn't have to get to $30 to make money on the option. Depending on the time left to expiration, your option could double to $1.50 , then go to $2.50 on a one or two dollar down-tick in the stock. You can sell at a profit anytime, and you can sell the option anytime before it expires.

Now check the $40 put. (To check if one exists, see if a bid and an ask are being written.) It might be going for 6¹/₂ x 6³/₄ bid and ask. Think of this: The stock is at $34³/₄. It's $5.25 in the money ($40 strike price minus $34.75 = $5.25). Part of your put option premium is intrinsic value ($5.25). The balance is time value. You're paying $1.50 ($6.75 - $5.25 = $1.50) for time. This is also referred to as extrinsic value. It's what you're paying for the time needed for this stock to do something.

103

This strike price is so far in the money that the relationship between the stock movement and the option movement may be in close ratio. (See Delta Formula in the **Wall Street Money Machine**.) The stock goes to $33 and your $6.75 option goes to $8. (A $1.75 downward movement in the stock increases your option value of $1.25 up to $8.) Now the stock goes to $30 and your option is worth $11. A nice relationship—a nice profit. Sell it for a nice gain. Even if the stock continues down you have a nice profit. (If you still think it hasn't hit bottom and you still have time before the expiration date, you may want to wait and try to get $12 or $13.) You'll kick yourself if the stock starts back up. As the stock price rises, the value of your $11 put option decreases.

Take the profit and use some of it to buy a $30 or $35 call option, or get in on a different play.

1) Options are a fixed time investment.

2) You should be doing this with money you can afford to lose.

3) You should choose a month far enough out for the stock to perform as you hope.

I really like in-the-money options, but not too far in the money. The $40 put in the last example looked nice, but to double our money we need a large movement in the stock. $6.75 to $12 or $13 requires a stock at $27 or $28.

Stock Price	$30 put	$35 put	$40 put
$34.75	$1 .50	$3.00	$6.75
34.00	1.25	3.375	7.25
33.00	1.75	4.00	8.125
32.00	2.50	4.75	9.00
30.00	4.00	6.50	10.50
28.00	6.00	7.875	12.50
27.00	6.75	8.75	13.50

No, I don't have to double my money on the option to be happy—a 20% to 40% profit in a few days is just fine—but it is a calculation I make in my head. Some stockbrokers have a computer model which gives a "% to double" to see how much of a movement is needed in the time available.

The $35 put and the $30 put require much smaller movements to be profitable. Look at the previous diagram to see a comparison.

Look at the tremendous leverage in the $30 put. Obviously you can lose if the stock doesn't move way down, and obviously there's some safety in the $40 put—because it's so far in the money, but you get your greatest bang for the buck on the cheaper options.

Also note: in rare cases there may be $32.50 puts and $37.50 puts. You could check and see.

Next point: You should check the option price for several different expiration dates. Look at your charts and make sure you give the stock/option plenty of time to move. If it goes through adverse swings, you still have time to recover.

What if the value of your option goes down? You have three choices:

1) Wait it out (perhaps get in your order to sell at a price you like, so you don't have to check on it every day).

2) Sell it at a loss and lose all or some of your money.

3) Buy more at the lower price. Jump back in if you still like the story.

EXAMPLES:

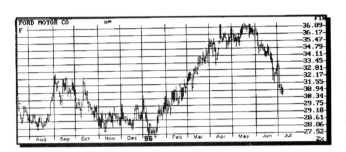

Ford (F): Rolls between $27 and $33. At the time this chapter was written it had broken out to $35. Maybe it will go back down, or maybe it will establish a new roll range or climb to an all time high.

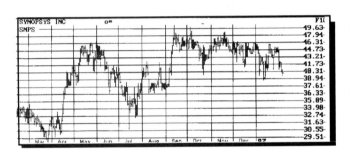

Synopsys (SNPS): This has been a personal favorite. Before it split (2:1) in the summer of '95, it was rolling almost weekly between $56/$57 and about $64/$66. It was incredible. Since the split it has established several ranges. $32 to $36 and $28 to $32, and $38 to $42.

Gaylord Container (GCR): We've used this as a covered call stock also. Very good. Look at the roll range between $8 and $11.

Microsoft (MSFT) is so often in the news that it's a natural. When this chapter was written it was rolling between $98 and

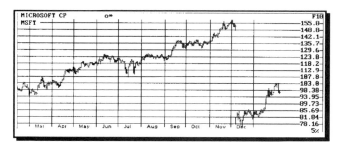

$104. This has been a great cash flow machine. I wish it would never quit—except for perhaps a new stock split just seconds after it dips and I've loaded up on call options—well, I can have dreams, too.

FORMULA #3—PEAK PROFITS

Buying put options when a stock has had a tremendous run up will have the same timing, and the same in-the-money, and out of the money pricing as a rolling option which has peaked. However, there is one substantial difference and this difference can make you a lot of money—very quickly.

Here is how it works. Every day there are several stocks which close several dollars higher. They usually move higher on news. Sometimes, but very seldom, they do so for no reason whatsoever. The good news is usually about earnings—and if the earnings are great, the new high might be sustained, but if it's something other than earnings, i.e. a takeover, a merger, new product, stock split, etc., the news can play out very quickly.

As in the "Dead Cat Bounce" strategy, the Peak Strategy happens very quickly. You have to be ready to move—not only on the purchase but also to sell. I usually know my exit (sell price) when I get involved.

There are so many examples it is difficult to only choose three or four for this chapter. There are sometimes hundreds a day. I go for the big moves, so let's show you how to do this, right after we explain the play.

A stock goes up $8 in one day—on whatever news. It goes from $52 to $60 between 2:30 P.M. and closing at 4:00 P.M. (Eastern Time.). It stops right around $60. We wait. There may be additional good or bad news after the market closes. If you think it has peaked, buying it now might be the move.

The next morning we check the news; we see the direction of the stock—waiting for resistance, or a good top. Usually this means the stock starts moving back down. This top may take several days to establish. The $8 run up was great but it goes up $2 the next day and then about noon on the third day, after it's gone up another dollar, it gives back that $1 and even drops another 50¢.

If you think the news has played out, consider buying the $60 put or the $65 put. Let's say the $65 put is going for $4 (the stock is at $62.50) while the $60 put is $1. Then over the next several weeks or months the stock gives back one-half of the $10 plus run-up. Your put value will grow drastically.

I usually buy these out a month or two. If I do them short term—two weeks to six weeks—I usually do in-the-money options ($65 put). If I play out further and there is no new news on the horizon (earnings reports won't be out for another three months, etc.), I'll play out-of-the-money puts— say $60 or even the $55 put if I'm feeling wild.

EXAMPLES:

1) Last year Chey-
enne Software
(CYE) was to
come out with
great earnings.
The price of the
stock started to
move up. Later

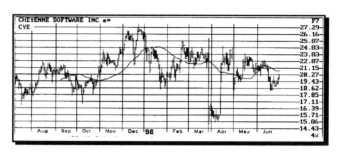

they announced a multi-hundred-million-dollar write-off
from some bad deal. The stock went down the next day.

2) F a n n i e
Mae (FNM) an-
nounced a 4:1
stock split.
Later it an-
nounced a bil-
lion-dollar
stock buy back.

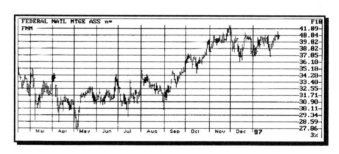

3) Intel (INTC) an-
nounced a
stock split,
then within
days, they an-
nounced an in-
crease in their
dividend.

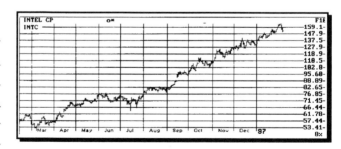

The list is endless. I believe we live in a very short-term society. We forget good news in about three days. It takes three months to forget bad news. This is only my conjecture, "the gospel according to Wade." I have no empirical evidence to back up the three day/three month statement, only a string of profitable trades using this as a guideline.

EXAMPLES:

Yes, you can make money on both up and down stock movements. Use these strategies for maximum cash flow.

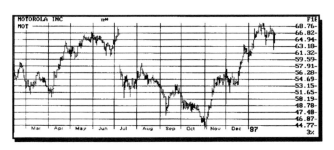

Motorola (MOT): a longtime favorite rolling stock (not rolling, now) shot up $6 in one day. We had call options and sold out at a nice profit. Then when it peaked, we rode it back down.

United Airlines (UAL) announced a 4:1 split. It shot up. We got in and out. Then when it peaked at $220, we got in on the puts. There was still plenty of time before the split date—it went down.

Author's note: Just because a stock splits doesn't mean it immediately starts climbing up. Sometimes there's a sell off (or whatever) and the stock goes down. See how to play these movements under Stock Splits.

DIFFERENT PEAK PLAYS

A) Earnings news. Many company stocks have a 5% to 10% jump on good earnings news. Be careful, however. Sometimes earnings are up but the stock goes down. This usually occurs when the earnings are not as good as some analysts projected. This news plays out really fast. Many people buy the stock in hopes of a better dividend. The short run up is truly short. The stock doesn't always go back down to where it was before the last bit of news, but many times I've seen it go lower. I think the reason for this is that the stock was already up in anticipation of good news (company leaks, press speculation, etc.). There usually is no long-term stability for the "jumped up" higher price. Rather, the direction is down. This is one of my favorite formulas. Why? Because we make money so fast.

B) Mergers, Acquisitions—especially failed attempts when companies take over other companies. I usually like to play the one being taken over. If the attempt fails, or takes longer than expected, the stocks go down—witness Chrysler (C) a while ago. There are two plays:

1) If there is a lot of debt involved (especially acquisition of new debt), as compared to a stock swap, the bigger company's (the one doing the takeover or merger) stock may see a quick—usually small—run up and then come down as investor euphoria cools. Sometimes the terms of the deal have a chilling effect.

2) The baby company's stock may run up to the take over price but quickly cool with the lapse of time. This may be time for call options (not put options) if the takeover is friendly and the price is right.

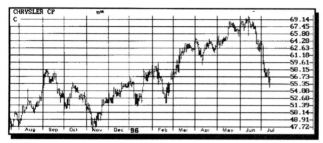

C) Spin-offs: When a big company spins off a division or subsidiary and a lot of cash is to be generated, there is usually a nice up tick in the stock. From my experience, though, it is short-lived. Why? The company selling off usually has other problems (the core business is in trouble) and the directors are pressured by shareholder groups to liquidate assets to get the main business going or to distribute cash dividends, etc. The problems don't go away easily and the stock dribbles back down.

D) Stock splits: Stock splits offer so many opportunities, I cannot do justice to them here. I've written extensively on them in the *Wall Street Money Machine* and I do so many plays (with explanations) on our Computer Bulletin Board Service (W.I.N. = Call 1-800-872-7411 for details). We'll just deal with the put play in this chapter.

The key is to watch and wait. If the stock runs way up on the announcement of the stock split and continues to climb on other good news announcements like an increase in dividends, just be patient. It will probably take a dip.

REMEMBER:

1) The stock is probably entering new territory—it may be ripe for a sell off as investors take their profits.

2) There are whole market swings, or at least sector swings (sympathy moves?) to contend with.

3) Other news—competition from others, charge offs, etc., may affect the stock.

Remember most stocks just don't go up in a straight line. Wait for true strength, check your charts (stochastic, market sentiments, etc.) and ride the stock down with a put option. Look at the following examples:

Accustaff (ASTF) was an awesome play. Many of our investors and students found this easy. Calls on 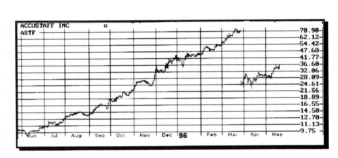 dips, puts on strength. For a short time it was a roller.

McDonnell Douglas (MD) announced a 2:1 split. It had a nice steady increase going. Then the whole market went down (first part of April, 1996) and Mc-Donnell Douglas went down too. 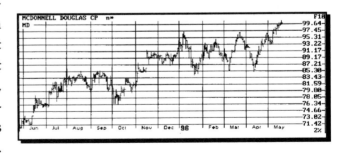 When it hit $94, with almost two months left before the split I figured it was too high. It did go down to $88, then it became a call candidate once again.

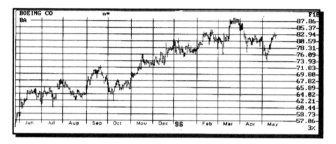

Boeing (BA) also climbed close to $90. When it hit $88, I bought the $90 puts at $2 7/8 on April 17, and sold the $85 calls for a large profit.

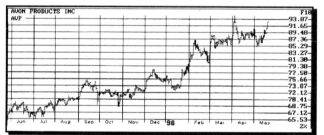

Avon (AVP) had a steady incline line, almost too good to be true. When it got into the low $90's, I thought it peaked. The $90 puts were the play.

Here are some other charts for your perusal. The point of putting these here is to show volatility.

Now look what happens after the split. Sometimes they go up and level off, but sometimes they go down.

Wait for weakness.

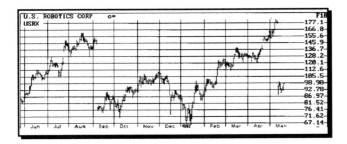

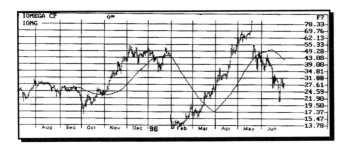

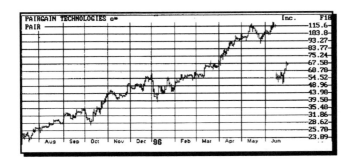

Sometimes the stock goes nowhere. It may be so high before the split that there is nowhere to go in the short term (usually due to stockholders selling off to lock in their gains) so the stock falls. These are hard to time. I usually wait for weakness and buy the call before I start playing puts. I want it to establish a roll pattern or run up to a new high. In short: to play puts we need all indicators pointing to a decrease in the stock price.

Selling Puts

I've written on this in another chapter entitled "Selling Puts." But in this chapter on puts, it is necessary to mention the gist of the strategy.

Like calls, puts can be bought and sold. Up until now, this chapter has only dealt with buying puts—then selling (closing out a position) on puts we've previously purchased.

Now let's explore selling put options we don't own. If buying a put gives us the right to put the stock to someone else, then selling this right would allow someone to put the stock to us. We would have an obligation to purchase the stock. (This is the exact opposite of writing a covered call.)

Why would we do this? Two reasons.

1) To generate cash. When we sell a put we get that premium into our account tomorrow.
2) We want to own the stock at a lower price, or at least be willing to buy it at the put strike price.

I love this strategy. An example would be in order. A stock is at $13.50. It's been rolling between $12 and $15 but you think it may break out and go way up.

You sell the October (one or two months out) $15 put for $3.50, or the $12.50 put for $1. One contract would generate $350, the other $100. Ten contracts would get you $3,500 or $1,000.

What have you done? You've agreed to let someone sell you the stock at $15. (We'll just use the $15 strike price for the balance of this example.)

If the stock stays below $15, you will get it put to you. But think: Your cost basis is $11.50 because you received $3.50 from the put premium. You bought the stock wholesale.

If the stock goes above $15 (remember this is what you thought would happen), the put option becomes increasingly worthless—you get to keep the premium and you don't have to buy the stock. Why would they sell it to you for $15 if it can be sold on the open market for $16 or more.

OR BUY A CALL?

If you think the stock is going up, why not buy a call option? My standard answer is, "You can do that too." Think about it. You've bought a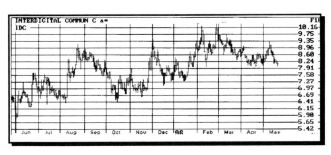

call and sold a put on the same stock. Why both, or why sell the put? Simply because selling generates income. Buying costs money. It's a way of getting more cash into your account more quickly. Look at Interdigital Communications (IDC) and Gaylord Container (GCR). There are too many to list.

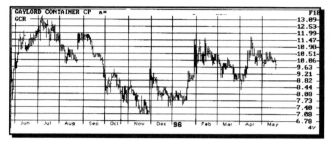

The only hang-up is this. Many beginners reading this chapter will not be allowed to sell naked puts (a covered put would be a situation where you're in a short position on the underlying stock) until you have more experience and/or more cash in your account. You see, you have the obligation to perform if the stock is put to you so your broker will require you to keep that amount of money (or 20% plus if you are on margin) on hold until the expiration date.

> *Selling puts generates income and lets you buy the stock wholesale.*

If you are just getting started, you may want to stick to call options. I did and it worked for me quite nicely. But once you get familiar with rolls, peaks and valleys and predictable stock movements, the put option tool gives you a way to truly enhance your income stream. Indeed, you can make twice as much as you catch the stock coming and going.

8

How To Get A Free Ride, Sort Of...

How would you like to get your stock investments for nothing? I'm not saying nothing down, but nothing, as in zero, zilch, nada. If you had no money tied up in an option purchase and you made $8,000, what would your rate of return be? For the answer to this question, figure out the answer to this division problem: $8,000 divided by 0 = ?. You say, "You can't divide by zero." Exactamundo. If you understand this, your work in real life will take on new meaning. The stars will shine brighter, your marriage will be happier, your kids will mind you, and you'll golf a 68.

Something For Nothing

Something for nothing? Sounds impossible. Well, there are many wild and crazy impossibilities coming down everyday. This chapter is full of possibilities—infinite possibilities. As a matter of fact, the rate of return above is infinite because you can't divide nothing into anything. It is physically impossible to divide nothing into something. Go ahead—try!

Let's talk money. You calculate a rate of return based on dividing the profits (gain) by your investment. A $1,200 profit on a $10,000 investment is 12%. That's simple. Now let's take on a hard one. A $1,200 profit on a zero dollar investment, produces an infinite rate of return. The trick, my dear Sherlock, is getting $1,200 out of nothing.

Would you like to know that it's just not that tough? We're not going to defy gravity or any other law of nature. We'll just defy the laws of stodgy-thinking, Wall Street insiders who are helplessly locked into boring investment strategies. We are going to take all or some of our profits and buy or continue to own some of the stock. It's that simple, and while not exactly free, it has that semblance.

MULTIPLE OPPORTUNITIES

There are many opportunities in stock and option investing to get a free ride—ownership of an investment which costs nothing. It may have taken a shrewd play to make the profits needed to now have ownership in an option or stock with no outlay—or, at least having all your initial investment returned and ready to go to work again. The process of making back your initial outlay and then using profits to stay in the game is "Infinity Investing." Remember, you cannot divide by zero. It is physically impossible. If you have no cash tied up, you will make an infinite return. Also, if you have no cash tied up, you can't lose—except to the extent that you have an opportunity lost in that your money might have done better elsewhere. Obviously, there is a cost because you could have moved the money elsewhere. Your cost is "what else could you have done?"

For the strategies in this chapter, we begin with the assumption that your investment in stocks or in options (either calls or puts) has grown in value, at least enough of an increase to cover the spread between bid and ask—in short, to be profitable. Now we are going to sell all or part of the investment. What we do with this profit and the calculated returns is our topic. Let's start with stocks.

WHY DID YOU BUY?

For this next section to make sense you need to know why you bought the stock.

Was it . . .

- a new start-up and/or a new IPO?
- a bottom fishing stock, i.e. one having a serious dip in price?
- a rolling stock and you know the roll range (the channel between support and resistance)?
- purchased for a covered call strategy?
- a high quality stock added to your portfolio for strength?

If you don't know why you got involved, it will be difficult to ascertain the best time to sell. Indeed, except for the last point above, in all the other strategies the "exit" is more important than the "entrance." Remember, my rock-bottom investment strategy is to build up your cash flow.

This last statement has gotten me into hot water with a lot of traditionalists around the country. There are the investment clubs, the old-time brokerages, and even journalists who can't bring themselves to try anything new. The Warren Buffett philosophy is rampant. Don't get me wrong, I love his strategy. After you have mastered your own cash flow strategies and have built up your income, start concentrating on building a solid portfolio of "keepers."

Two points:

1) If you have a substantial portfolio and seriously want more income, then take a few thousand dollars and try more aggressive strategies. Call it play money. (Note: Most of our Wall Street Workshop attendees with substantial assets have and do make more profits by taking $5,000 of their $100,000 and investing it in rolling stocks, rolling options, option plays on stock splits, slams, peaks, et cetera, than they make on the other $95,000. Sure their $95,000 is safe and growing nicely. Just think, $95,000 at 10% will produce just under $10,000. But, I've seen a lot of people (too many to count) take $5,000 and make over $250,000 a year. And, not quite so obvious, this is actual cash flow, not just an increase in value. It's time to head for the Bahamas.

2) If you only have a few thousand to invest, then you may want to throw caution to the wind and go for the gusto. If that's where you are in your life and you want to generate income quickly, most mutual funds, stocks, and bonds will not respond fast enough. It's time to put a formula (system, recipe) to work and quickly "get in and get out." It's the <u>formula</u> that works, not a particular stock.

YOUR VANTAGE POINT

This concept will not become real to you without the following two aspects.

1) You know going into an investment exactly what you want out of it.

2) You have purchased your investment wholesale—on a serious low in the stock (and, hence, the option.)

Let's get on to a real life example. When you get to the option section, coming up in a few pages, this will get even more exciting.

You buy a stock for $8. It has been as high as $20. It's been down to $6. Lately it's been trading between $7 and $11. You buy 1,000 shares for $8,000. It takes three months, but the stock goes to $12. Your value is $12,000.

Now, should you . . .

1) Sell it all and then hope it goes back down, and then buy in again?

    A little voice speaks up: "But what if it goes to $30? After all, that's what the analysts say."

    OR

2) Hold on?

    Another little voice speaks up, "But what if it goes back to $7?"

    OR

3) Sell part of it—in fact recapturing all your investment, then ride the remainder to greater returns?

FIREWORKS, ORCHESTRA, FANFARE—BINGO— YOU'VE GOT IT!

Sell 700 shares at $12. That generates $8,400. After taking out commissions for both trades, you should have your $8,000 back and look what you've done—the impossible. You own 300 shares of a $12 stock for zippo. Hopefully, this stock is in a great company. You have your cash back and 300 shares with no cash tied up.

I told you it wasn't that complicated or difficult. And there are still even greater things to think about. Before I delve into these I'd like to discuss a point. Many people, I'm sure, have thought of this, or at least have done it intuitively. Most powerful ideas are really quite simple.

I'm reminded of the story of the teacher who told all her first grade students that their drawing assignment that day was whatever they wanted to draw. As she was walking around the room checking on their progress, she saw one girl drawing intently. She asked what she was drawing. The youngster replied, " I'm drawing a picture of God."

"But no one knows what God looks like," the teacher said.

"They will when I get done," the girl said.

When you have profits now paying for your investment, and all your cash is out, then several things need to be discussed.

1) You can take your cash and wait and buy this same stock on a dip. Maybe next time you'll get 1,000 more shares at $7.

2) You can take your cash and buy a different, more promising opportunity.

3) The stock you still own (300 shares) is available for:

   A) Selling at a higher price.

   B) Writing a covered call—generating more income.

   C) Holding a good stock thereby increasing your margin account. 300 shares at $12 is $3,600. This could turn into $7,200 (on margin)—or another $3,600 in buying power.

4) If the stock goes down, it's a worry of course, but it didn't cost you anything.

5) If it goes up to the $20 range you could sell all of it, or part of it. Selling all would generate another $6,000.

No one knows what the picture will look like. You can draw it yourself, but you should also know what you want it to look like before you start drawing. Stay a step ahead by knowing what your investments will do for you.

What if you ignore this last piece of advice? What if you don't know why you purchased the stock? What if you purchased it just because your stockbroker told you to? What if you didn't check the charts to see the high and lows, the incline or decline, the range and time it takes to move from support to resistance? What if you haven't the foggiest idea of why you're in this stock?

Then how do you know when to get out, or buy more, or sell off part? You've got to know your exit before you go in the entrance!

One more point. If you know about this particular company, you've tracked its earnings, growth, etc. and you still like it—you still think it has potential, then:

1) The 300 shares you own may prove profitable.

2) You could buy call options at $10, $12.50 or $15. Again, use some profit (maybe sell 50 or 100 more shares) to buy these options.

3) If you wait for another dip, your chance of increasing your next returns will be quicker.

4) You could sell puts (see the chapter on selling puts) for more cash flow.

5) If you think the $12 is a high and it's going to go down, you could buy puts and sell them as they get profitable.

But what if the story (where you think the stock is heading) isn't very good? Yes, there's a chance it might go up and your 300 shares may get more valuable, but if the story line has lost its momentum, then looking for similar opportunities elsewhere may be more profitable.

By the way, a lot of people find my tapes and seminars very helpful when beginning to trade, or when learning to trade options. If you feel like you'd like some more information on the topics covered in this chapter, or in any of the other chapters in this book, please call the 1-800 number on the back of the book. We've put together some helpful free audio cassettes about these same stock market investment and asset protection strategies that I think are really great.

A lot of people tell me I'm crazy giving this kind of information away for free instead of writing another book and making people buy it. But I don't write books to make most of my money. I make most of my money from trading and doing business. I write books and give seminars because I truly believe that this is the kind of investment information everyone should be getting already from their stockbrokers or other financial advisors.

Anyway, look at the three graphs and explanations on the following page. They are staggered to prove a point. As the door closes on one opportunity it opens on another.

This stock went from $8 to $12. We sold at $12. The stock went nowhere. We felt $12 was the high. We were glad we did it, too, because the stock went nowhere for several months. We bought Perseptive Biosystems at $6 and...

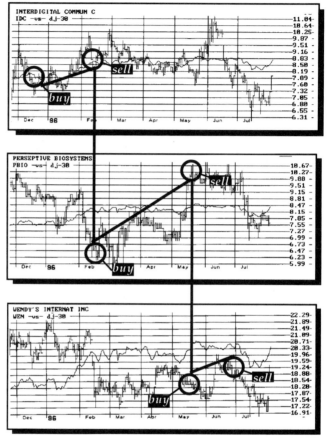

after a rise, then a decline, it went to $8. We sold at $10 and bought into Wendy's.

Wendy's stock was then purchased at $17 (near a bottom). We sold it at $19.

Again, you've got to decide if the play is over, then stay in or get out. There are always more opportunities.

Each time profits are created it gives you an opportunity for another free ride.

OPTIONS: PROXY INVESTING

Options (calls and puts) on stocks opens up all kinds of infinity-type returns and many ways to earn a free ride.

127

This is not the place to discuss all the aspects of options, but a few things are important to this discussion. Options allow you to control a large amount of stock with relatively small amounts of money. Also, small movements in the stock usually produce magnified movements in the option. Simply put, you can double, even triple your money, a lot faster. With these profits, a whole plethora of opportunities open up.

Remember though, we purchased the option for a specific purpose and at/for a specific time.

1) CALL OPTIONS (We think the stock will rise). The stock is...

   A) rolling

   B) on a dip (slam, bottom fishing)

   C) doing a split

   D) coming out with news

2) PUT OPTIONS (We think the stock will go down). The stock has...

   A) bad news

   B) a reverse split

   C) peaked out—run up on good news, unsustainable

   D) come within a few days of the split date (give or take two to eight days)

Let's stick with call options for this example. Put options are the same but in reverse. The above is for <u>purchasing</u> calls and puts. Selling them is a whole different story.

The stock is at $40. It has traded as high as $50 and has been down to $38. You think it has potential. It seems to have bottomed out in the high $30 to low $40 range. It's August. You purchase 10 contracts of the October $40 calls for $3.75; your cost is $3,750. You also purchase 10 contracts of the January $45 calls for $4.25. Total outlay is $4,250. By September 8 the stock is at $44. Your October $40 calls are $6.25, or $6,250. The January options are up also, but because they're further out they haven't moved as much. They are $5.75— still a $1,500 profit.

Now what do you do? Check again why you bought the options. If you're following the Wade Cook method, it was not to purchase 2,000 shares of this stock. But wait. What do I see? A nice quick profit—extra cash generated in hours or days.

Look what you can do with these profits. Let's just deal with the October calls.

1) Continue to hold for greater profits.

2) Sell some—say eight contracts for $6.25. That's about $5,000. We have all our cash back and we can even take some profits and buy more options on this stock or other stocks. In this case we would only have to sell 7 to recover our investment and get a FREE RIDE on the other three.

    Note: If this run-up of $4 (10% of the stock price) had occurred in a one or two day period, I'd probably sell all of the options. Barring additional news, most of these quick spurts are not sustainable. Sell, then buy back in on a dip at an expiration date a little further out. The October options were purchased in August. If it's now mid-September we should probably look at the November or December options.

3) Sell all or part of the options and buy some of this stock.

This point is very important to me. I've written on it elsewhere but it is also appropriate here. I am big into building a solid portfolio of well-run companies with good earnings and hopefully increasing earnings. I like companies with expansion dynamics at work. Most people who read my books and come to my seminars need more cash flow. They, like me in the beginning, need a more aggressive approach with a small amount of money. They need to develop their own money machine.

Then they should diversify into real estate, gold, or other investments like small businesses, energy resources, etc. The stock market is too risky for all your money to be in one basket. Some of this diversification could be into stocks in great companies—even recession-proof companies. Get back to fundamentals and doing your homework.

Speaking of homework, part of the homework you did to decide if you wanted this option in the first place—and which option (strike price, expiration date), will now help you decide if you should buy or sell this stock, or hold on to it.

Remember, if we've sold ten October contracts for $6.25, that's $6,250, of which $2,500 is profit. Yes, we could take all of this money ($6,250) and buy more options, but if you follow this thought, your portfolio will be full of risk. Options expire. Be careful. A downturn in the market could wipe out a substantial part of your assets.

Let's use all of the $2,500 or even half of it, and buy some stock. If you like the $44 stock, buy 10 shares, or 50, or even

100. One hundred shares would cost $4,400, but only $2,200 on margin.

You're free riding again. Your $2,500 is put to a good, yes boring, but still a good use. Use your $3,750 (your option/ profit seed money) for your next quick play.

There is an advantage to owning stock in a lot of companies. One is that shareholders receive news from the companies: updates, reports, and shareholder voter information. Get them, read them. You're learning about earnings, expansion plans, stock splits, changes in management, etc. Part of good investment habits is to get, and act upon, good and timely information. Shareholders get this all the time.

MORE OPTIONS

If you want to play more options on this same company, consider the following:

Wait for dips—be patient. Study the charts and pick the most opportune strike price and expiration date.

Sell out, take your profits, and buy back in at a higher strike price. Once again the assumption has to be that the stock will increase.

Opportunities keep knocking when you have no cash tied up.

Selling the option profitably opens up another possibility. If you sell part of your position, and if you think the stock has peaked (you still own a few call options) then buy a put with the profit. You now have created a straddle for FREE.

A pure straddle is one where you own calls and puts on the same stock at the same strike price and for the same month. Your straddle does not have to be pure. You can buy a call at one strike price, and buy a put at another strike price.

Either way, as the stock moves up you sell the call, as the stock moves down you sell the put. Something for nothing, I can't add more. It's a great way to enhance your cash flow and/or add to your portfolio.

9

Knowing When To Sell

Never before has it taken so long for me to write a chapter. I've had my notes ready, with few additions, for months. Why? Because this information is so vital, so pertinent, that I wanted plenty of time to think and time to formulate answers to all the questions I get about the timing of sell points.

How To Know When To Sell

I have given a lot of this information elsewhere: bits and pieces here, brief explanations there. It is probably the most visited area of all my seminars and personal meetings: "When do I get out (sell)?" I think people ask me this because from my real estate days on, I've advocated several generalized exit strategies, including:

1) Know your exit before you go in the entrance.

2) You capitalize your profits when you sell.

I've also made remarks like the following: "It's easy to get into business; it's hard to get out. It's easy to buy real estate; it's hard to sell. It's easy to get into personal relationships with people; it's hard to get out. It's always easier to get in than to get out, but you make your money when you get out.

Sure, you have to buy right going in (and if you do you'll make a profit), but again, you get the cash (or cash flow) when you sell."

Also, I mentioned to people at my real estate seminars that I felt sorry for them if they asked me a question about a problem they were having with their properties because I only had one answer: sell.

The reader must also understand my "cabdriver" mentality background.

1) The money is made in the meter drop. You make more by ending one run quickly and getting on to the next. I know this is contrary to all the current advice. I, too, buy and hold some stocks. But the cash flow comes from buying and selling—trading, and getting on to the next deal.

2) There's always another cab (or bus or train). I once read an old Irish proverb that makes sense here: "The biggest fish you'll ever catch is still swimming in the ocean." I'll add, "you've got to be out fishing to catch it."

Remember, my style is to turn the stock market into a business. No business buys inventory to keep. The profits are in the selling process.

With all this in mind let me move on to the strategies that have helped me get rich. Remember, I use various formulas and processes, rules, if you will, to get me in and out. Each has a distinctive nature, and only occasionally are the rules the same. For example, selling a call on a covered call play is totally different than selling stock on a rolling stock play.

This chapter is about exiting. Obviously there will be more on getting into the stocks in the various other chapters on these formulas.

Let's start with my old favorite, rolling stock.

ROLLING STOCK

This one is easy because you can run a chart (go back six months, a year or even five years) and see the peaks and valleys. You look at the high point (it's formally called "resistance") and put your order in to sell at that point or just below that point: remember, don't get greedy.

A stock may roll between $3 and $4.50, but it only hits $4.50 once in a while. Put your order in to sell at $4.25. You'll probably want to put in a "Good Till Cancelled" (GTC) order (and renew it if the sixty days expire). Look at the following charts:

You can see in Royal Oak Mines (RYO) that the roll range changes. Most people freak out if the stock goes down—especially after they just bought it. Only once in a while have I been burned by this. You see, you have two choices. First though, look at a changing roll pattern with Cineplex Odeon (CPX).

For years (this is a one year chart) it has gone between $2.50 and $3.50. Then it dropped to $1.50. I had just purchased 2,000 shares at $2.50 and then another 2,000 at $2 when it

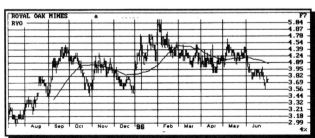

dropped to the $1.50 range. It even hit $1.25 once or twice. Now the two choices:

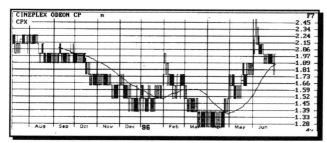

1) Just wait it out. It may take several months for it to get back up to $3 or $3.50. But at least you won't lose.

2) Hang on to what you have and wait to see if it establishes a new roll range. A variation of this is to look for a significant bottom, real support and a genuine move back up in the stock. That's what I did. I bought some at $1³/₈ and $1¹/₂ and sold most at $1⁷/₈ and a little at $2. It went back to $1¹/₂ or so and I bought back in.

As we were going to press with this chapter it looked like Cineplex Odeon (CPX) was establishing a new roll range. I'll make more cash flow on quick rolls than anything I'd lose on the dip in value of the 4,000 shares. Plus, I still have the 4,000 shares with two more choices:

1) Continue to hang on.

2) Sell, take the loss, and get the cash moving on this lower roll range, or invest elsewhere.

Your Order To Sell

You can either place a GTC order and forget about it, or you can watch it closely and sell at an optimum time. Which method you use depends upon you; more specifically, on how busy you are. If you're really busy, just place the GTC order and get on with your other business. If you have ample time, you'll probably make more by watching the stock and figuring out the best time to sell.

Also note, on any given day the stock could move in tandem with the whole stock market. At least it could give it an extra 25¢ to 50¢ of profitability. For example: Let's say a stock is rolling between $3 and $4. It hits $4.50 once in a while. You have a GTC order to sell at $4. The past few days it has run up quickly to $3.75 and the market is strong. Consider cancelling your GTC order and watch it, or change it to $4.25 or $4.50. No, it's not getting greedy, it's just smart. The economy, or good news, or an up Dow could drive it up to its high or even beyond.

Conversely, a down market may drive the price to $2.50 or $2.75. If you buy now, you pick up an extra 25¢ to 50¢ when you sell at $4. It's not only a bargain but a super bargain.

In December of 1995, I had been intrigued by the reported returns in the mailers from Wade Cook Seminars. I had not made a commitment to attend the Wall Street Workshop but decided to "just try" a rolling stock strategy to see if it really worked. Wade had touted Cineplex Odeon (CPX) as a rolling stock. January 4th 1996, I bought (on margin) 2,000 shares of CPX at 1^1/_2$ and placed an order to sell at 2^1/_2$.

A month later, I was less excited when they hadn't reached 2^1/_2$ and I adjusted my sell per share to $2. I decided to attend the Chicago WSWS in June. While I was there, CPX increased to $2 and my sell order was executed. The results were great.

—Steven M.

All Or Part

You can also sell part of your position at one price and part at another. If you bought 1,000 shares at $3, you could place your GTC order on 500 shares at $4 and 500 shares at $4.25.

This is obviously personal to you. I can't begin to tell you what to do, just as I can't tell you all the ramifications of what you can do.

ROLLING OPTIONS

Exiting a position on rolling options is quite similar to a plain rolling stock play. If you find a stock which rolls (channels) within a certain range, and if the stock is optionable, then as it hits its low figure you purchase a call option at the next higher strike price. If it's a stock under $25, you may want to purchase it two strike prices higher.

EXAMPLE: A stock rolls between $18 and $22. When it gets to $18 and bottoms out, purchase the $20 call. Its price is 62.5¢. Ten contracts would cost $625. Now wait or put in your GTC order to sell. Try to guess when to get out. After you've done it several times you'll just know a good exit point. If the stock hits $21 (remember don't get greedy) and the option then goes for $1.50 you could sell for $1,500 and have a cool $875 profit. Nice and predictable.

If the stock has frequently bumped against, and even gone over $22.50 (the next higher strike price), you may want to purchase the option at that strike price. It would be really cheap if the stock were $18. How does 12.5¢ ($^{1}/_{8}$) sound? If you go to the next higher strike price, you should probably consider going out one or two additional months.

Instead of 12.5¢ the option may be 37.5¢, but that additional quarter may well be worth it. And frankly, the stock may need more time to get close to, or over, the $22.50 strike price.

Realize also, you're not doing this to buy the stock. You're doing this play to wait for an increase in the value of your option so you can sell at a profit. Now where do you sell? Probably the same place as before—in the $21 plus range. It won't take too much of a move for you to double or even triple your money. And again you could have a GTC order in place or watch and wait and sell at an optimum time.

THE WAY DOWN

If you choose to purchase puts on the way down, do everything in reverse. Wait for the stock to peak out, check for other news, including where the market in general is heading (don't fight trends), and buy a put. Sell it as the stock decreases in value. On a $25 stock, purchase the $22.50 put or even consider the $25 or $20. The $25 put will cost more because it's in the money, but you have some insurance. The $20 (or lower) strike price will cost less because it's way out of the money. Pick an exit point that you're comfortable with and upon selling the put, watch for the true bottom (or support level) to sell the put, then jump back in with a call option and ride it back up. Keep the cycle going.

Date (Expiration Friday, Nov. 19)	Stock Price	Option Price on $25 Call
Oct. 20	$26.00	$1.75
Oct. 25	27.00	3.00
Oct. 30	28.00	4.25
Nov. 5	29.00	5.50
Nov. 10	31.00	6.75
Nov. 15	32.00	7.625
Nov. 17	33.00	8.25
Nov. 19	34.00	9.125

I took the Wall Street Workshop in October of 1995. I bought options in a few companies and was ahead at the end of the year by a little over $9,000. You know, this year has been thrilling. My gains thus far in 1996 exceed $86,000! All of your courses have been wonderful, but your Wall Street Workshop has been the most rewarding financially. Thank you.

Sandi—Bellevue, Washington

OPTIONS: FOUR GENERAL SELL POINTS

A quick explanation would be in order. A stock option gives you a chance to purchase or sell an underlying stock. It's not a pure gamble in that you can actually act on the underlying security. Small movements in the underlying stock can produce, on a percentage basis, drastic moves in the option. I've seen a stock move up $3 and an option on that stock move up $2.50. You ask, so what? Well the stock went from $74 to $77. The $70 call option went from $5.25 to $7.75. Talk about a great proxy investment. The same can happen with puts.

Investors buy options for:

1) Maximum bang for your buck—the expiration month and various strike prices should be analyzed.

2) Quick return on your money.

Again, we're not here to discuss entrance strategies. You can read about those elsewhere. I only bring this up as a lead in to the next point. Is time a friend or foe? If we want to get out at not just a nice profit, but at the best possible profit, we need to explore this question.

An option may be comprised of two parts: intrinsic value and time value. Intrinsic value is that portion of the option which is in the money. Time value is that portion of the option which is out of the money. For example, if the stock is $26 and the $25 call options are going for $1.75, $1 of the $1.75 is intrinsic value and the 75¢ of the $1.75 purchase price is time value. 75¢ pays for one week or two months, or whatever time is left before the expiration date.

The reason I said "may" at the beginning of the last paragraph is that the option may be all time value. If you're after the $30 strike price, and the stock is at $26, and the option is 50¢, the whole 50¢ is time value. Time value could be called extrinsic value as it is extrinsic to the value of the stock.

At first, time is a friend. Your 75¢ has purchased you a month and a half—six weeks. If the stock rises, the option value increases. You could sell at anytime. If you had purchased a call option with a $30 strike price, the option value increases up to a point. If the stock goes above $30, you've made a nice play and you can get out at a nice profit.

If, however, the stock moves toward $30 and you've seen a nice run up in your op-

Stock Price	Date Expiration date: Fri, Nov 19	Option Price $30 call
$26.00	Oct. 20	50¢
$27.00	Oct. 25	75¢
$27.50	Oct. 30	$1.00
$28.00	Nov. 5	$1.25
$28.00	Nov. 10	$1.25
$28.25	Nov. 12	$1.375
$28.50	Nov. 14	$1.50
$28.75	Nov. 15	$1.50
$29.00	Nov. 16	$1.75
$29.25	Nov. 17	$1.75
$29.375	Nov. 18 *Thurs.*	$1.50
$25.43	Nov. 18 *noon Thurs.*	$1.37
$29.50	Nov. 19 *Fri.*	75¢
$29.50	Nov. 19 *noon Fri.*	25¢
$29.50	Expiration	worthless

tion, but then the stock stalls, you may want to be careful. Time becomes the enemy. The option (stock) needs time to move up, and more specifically, move to the strike price, or it may become worthless.

Look at the chart. Note the dates. Note how in the last few days before the expiration date the stock is still going up a little but the option goes nowhere and then down. Time runs out. We're purchasing the November $30 call options for 50¢.

Do you see how fast the time value deteriorates when there is no time left? As you look at this chart you can obviously see several exit points where you could have made a nice profit. Also note: the time value of in-the-money calls also evaporates as you get near the expiration date. Look at the chart. This is the $35 call option. The stock starts at $26.

Sometimes we, "tongue in cheek," refer to time value as fluff. When there is ample time before the expiration date, the time value portion of the option premium is large. In the above example it was 75¢ back on October 20, but only 25¢ two days before the November 19 expiration date.

Stock Price	Date Expiration: Fri., Nov. 19th	Option Price
$26.00	Oct. 20	75¢
27.00	Oct. 25	$1.00
28.00	Oct. 30	.75
29.00	Nov. 5	.75
31.00	Nov. 10	.50
32.00	Nov. 15	.25
33.00	Nov. 17	.25
34.00	Nov. 18	.125

There comes a time when you get less bang for your buck. I would have sold this option at a double or triple. Be careful. If it gets to be November 10 and the stock takes a two dollar dip, the value can erode very quickly.

When the stock has less time to recover it may not regain its previous value. A lot of money can be made in the expiration week but only for someone with a stout heart. I hope you see how easily the "friend" can quickly turn to "foe."

OUT OF YOUR OPTIONS

There are four major strategies for determining when to get out of options. I'll cover these as I blend in specific formulas on option plays. We'll look at:

- Peaks
- Slams ("Dead Cat Bounce")
- 90 degree angles
- Covered Calls
- Selling Calls
- Selling Puts
- Stock Splits

1) GET OUT WHEN YOU WOULDN'T GET IN

A lot of your investing will come down to how you feel. Your fears may keep you out of trouble. Your desire to get in when you hear great news will usually help you get great results. For example, all your research says a stock could hit $30 in a short time. It's currently $20. If it gets close to $28 you may want to sell. If you had purchased the $25 call option (or even the $30 option) and it's had a nice run, check the news, see if there's more potential upside and consider selling. If the stock is at $30 and no new news has come out, definitely sell.

Remember options have a short life. If you own the stock you could hang on and wait for the next earnings report or whatever. But you don't want the option to expire. Sell it and then buy back in at a higher strike price; or wait for weakness and buy back in at the same strike price—just out another month or two; or take your money elsewhere.

The point is this: If you wouldn't buy the stock or option at a certain price, and you do in fact own it, then sell it at that point where you wouldn't buy it. That sell point is your best-guess summation.

A variation of this point is using the "percent to double" or points to double rule which I've written about in the *Wall Street Money Machine*. We use the "%Dbl" to determine if buying an option is a good deal. Many brokers can get access to the on-line computer services which have this program. It's a computer model whose "bottom line" tells us how much a stock would have to move for us to double our money on a particular option. I like low percentage movements (under 10%)—take a quick profit and get out.

Let's say a stock is $82. The $90 strike price on the call option is $2.50 and the percent to double is 6%. The stock (at this particular point in time) would have to go up almost $5 for our $2.50 to double to $5. (6% of $82 = about $5). If the stock has an upward trend or good news, etc., then this could be a great play. Remember, your $2.50 option doesn't have to go up double for you to make a nice profit. A 50¢ move would be nice, especially if it's in a few days.

The point though, in this chapter is not to determine when to get in, but when to get out. If the stock and option have an upward move, check the %Dbl. If it's high, say 13%, then you should sell. Think of it: You probably wouldn't buy an option with a 13% to double. Back to our example: If the stock has moved to $88 and our $2.50 option is $4, and at this point (time remaining and other factors involved) it would require a $10 move to take the $4.50 to $9 then you may want to sell for the $4.50.

You'll probably get your biggest profits shortly after you've bought in at a really low price, then get out on a quick up-tick in the stock.

2) KNOW YOUR EXIT BEFORE ENTERING

I don't want to wear out this concept, but for many plays it's very important. Here we'll deal with a few option plays. We've already covered rolling options. Let's now cover a peak or a slam.

Peaks

When a stock has a tremendous run up, say in one day it goes from $52 to $63, because of good news, unless there's more good news coming out, it will probably back off. If you own the call options, get out. If you want to get in and play the downturn, buy puts on the stock and ride it back down. If the increase stalls, or even comes down a little, you could sell the options and buy back in on the dip.

If you own the stock, you could also write a covered call and again, ride it back down. You collect the premium and you also keep the stock.

Slams

When a stock takes a hit, you could buy a call and get out with a profit in hours. Here's how it works. The company comes out with lower than expected earnings (it's still highly profitable, but not up to what analysts expected). The stock falls from $62 to $54. The next day it finds support and even goes back up to $55. Consider buying the short term option and purchase the $55 call. It needs to be close. It's going for $2. (Note: the $50 call is $6: $5 in the money and $1 time value. This costs more but may be a better play. Think it through.) A move to $56 or $57 could easily drive your $2 option to $3. Then get out.

You could have gone further out (two to four months) on the $55 call or the $60 call but that was not this play. This is short term. You should have placed the order to sell at $3 (especially if you can't sit and watch it) right after you purchased it for $2. You know your exit before buying.

I have covered exit strategies on covered and uncovered calls and on selling puts elsewhere. I'll only add this here: They are options. They have a fixed life. If you've sold a call or put and generated cash you have two choices.

A) Let the option expire and keep the cash.

B) If the option shrinks significantly and you think the stock might bounce, then you could buy back the option and sell it again as it gets more profitable.

The best "out" enhancement strategy is to have gotten in at a bargain in the first place.

3) GET OUT WHEN YOU'RE HAPPY

I know this sounds ambiguous but it's important to realize that there is not just one time to get out. If you have invested $2,000 in ten contracts of a $2 option and one hour later it shoots up to $3 or $3,000, you have an hour profit of $1,000. If YOU'RE HAPPY, then get out. Take your profits and go to a movie.

Of course you shouldn't get out if there's more potential, but if this was initiated as a quick play, then take your profits and look for another deal—dips, new stock splits, etc. So what if it goes to $4. The next day it could be at 50¢.

Stocks and options are like ocean waves. They ebb in, they flow out. Nothing stays the same.

This is to let you know that during the five business days following the Wade Cook Wall Street Workshop, I averaged approximately $250 a day using only the covered calls technique I learned during the workshop. In addition, by working with a full-service broker, I was able to obtain a very good position in an IPO with excellent potential for a 100% gain on my money. Additionally, using the margin concept, I was able to obtain 500 shares of a strong "takeover" stock for a possible 30–40% profit.

All things considered, I am confident I have started on a realistic course to financial independence. Thanks to all in Kent for their time and expertise. Wade was correct when he said the workshop is worth more than 10 times the tuition amount.

Richard S.—Kent, Washington

4) WANGO

Most of my stockbrokers are so busy they won't do this strategy, however, the ones who really watch out for my best interests, will.

WANGO means Watch And Get Out. Let's say a stock is having a nice run up. You are quite profitable on your option but want to get out at maximum profit. Ask your stockbroker to keep an eye on it. If it peaks and you can catch it at or near the peak, then you can get out with an even greater return.

An example: The stock was at $80 after a slam, or other bad news, or even after good news. It goes to $81. You call your stockbroker and buy the $80 calls for $3 and the $85 calls for

$1.25. The stock goes to $83, then $84, and one hour before the market closes it's at $85—almost $86. The stock hangs around $86, seems to have stalled, backs off to $85.50 with 10 minutes before the close—this is it—(yes, there is tomorrow but this is today). Carpe diem. Seize the moment. Sell and take your profits. The $80 call is $6.25 and the $85 call is $3.75. That's a $3.25 profit on the $80's and a $2.50 profit on the $85's. It's been a nice day.

Yes, it may still go up tomorrow, but many times they fall back. This stock had a 3%, then 4%, then 5% run up in one day. Surely I can't tell you what to do, but I usually take my profits and wait for another dip.

Two more points:

A) The options market closes ten to fifteen minutes after the stock market. If you are willing to buy at the ask and sell at the bid (buy or sell at the market), you can still trade options at 4:05 P.M.., 4:10 P.M.., sometimes even 4:15 P.M.. Eastern time. Why do I bring this point up here? Many times, stocks go up or down a few dollars right at the close. If the options have a corresponding move, you could get out at a higher price or get in at a lower price.

However, unless there is really spectacular news (good or bad) which comes out over night, the options are usually pretty much the same the next morning. Just once in a while, I do option trades after the stock market closes.

B) If you have a good profit you could sell part of your position and keep part active. You don't have to sell all four contracts you've purchased. Sell part to capture some profits now and keep some to capture larger profits later.

You might even be profitable enough on the ones you've sold to regain all the money spent on all four contracts—you now own the two contracts you've kept, for free.

10

SELLING PUTS (MY FAVORITE STRATEGY)

Some of you have heard me tell the story of a certain gentleman in one of my early seminars who was disagreeing with me and dominating the seminar for two full days. Finally, someone asked me, "Wade, what is the single best investment strategy you know of? Where can you generate the richest returns?"

I saw the chance to make a point, so I turned to my heckler and handed him the question. He said, "Easy. Sell puts." And then I said, "I agree, but now aren't you people glad you paid me to teach you investment strategies instead of attending this man's seminar, because he would have spent two days teaching you to sell puts, and you would have gone home and discovered you couldn't do it. You can't sell puts until you have both a lot of experience and/or a substantial reserve of cash set aside in your account."

Well, people have always been grateful that we teach them eleven strategies at our seminars which they can implement immediately to generate cash flow. And many of our students have done just that. In fact, they have gained so much experience and generated so much cash that they are ready now to sell puts! And so the time has come for this chapter.

THE BASICS OF SELLING PUTS

It's about cash flow and a rather unique way of getting it. Everyone has heard that you can make money in any market, but the people saying so fail to give details on how to do it. More specifically, "they" say you can make money whether a stock is going up or coming down. I want to give some specifics on how to make money in options where the stock is increasing or decreasing in value. This is an option chapter. We will explore a cash flow generation strategy which will deal with stocks that you hope are going up—or will at least stay the same. Note: See the chapter "Tandem Plays" for doubling up these strategies.

Selling (naked) puts is a very unique and seldom-used strategy with a host of benefits. We will put some flesh on this skeleton, and some muscle, give it a brain and put it to work for you.

Definitions are in order. Stock option investing gives an investor the right, but not the obligation to buy or sell a particular stock at a set price (strike price) on or before a certain date. Call options give the investor the right to buy a stock. These options can be bought or sold. Put options give the investor the right to sell a stock. They, too, can be bought or sold.

Strike prices for all options are the same. They start at $5, and go up by $2.50 increments to $25, in $5 increments to $200 and in $10 increments thereafter. Options are written in 100 share contracts. Hence, a 75¢ option will cost $75 for one contract. Options are derivatives. A derivative is a proxy investment based on an underlying security. Stock options are different than most derivatives in that the investor actually has the right to take control of (own by purchasing or selling) the underlying stock.

Options end—they expire. Because they are a fixed-time investment, investors should not only be wary and very cautious, but should invest in options by keeping an eye on the time clock. You may have the best horse on the track but if it falls behind or gets a bad start, the race may be over before it begins. The price of the option is broken into two parts. Part of the premium is actually purchasing the time until the option expires. This is called time value. If the stock price is above the strike price (call options) or below the strike price (put options), the option is said to be "in-the-money." That portion of the option which is in the money is called intrinsic value. I will use several examples and this definition will come to life. Understanding time value (extrinsic) and intrinsic value is not only important, but *sine qua non* to effectively making decisions on which option to purchase on a particular stock.

Put options, and a particular angle to using them, is the topic here. Let's keep exploring them. If you purchase a put option, you are thinking (hoping) that the stock will go down. What if, however, you don't think the stock is going down? In fact, you think the stock is a winner. Is buying the stock or buying a call option on the stock the only way to take advantage of an increasing stock value?

No, selling puts is another strategy which accomplishes two major objectives:

1) It generates new income.

2) If you have to buy the stock, it lets you buy wholesale.

There are other minor strategies which allow for even greater returns. We'll get to those later.

On Monday, July 8, I heard that Ascend Communications was going to announce their quarterly earnings this week. Well, I've been waiting for an opportunity to buy some shares. I have traded this stock many times and I know it is one of Wade's favorites. Lately the stock has broken its upward trend pattern and retreated from its high of $71.25 in late May. I felt this might be a good buy here in the $55 range, but still wanted to hedge a little. I would be delighted to buy the stock at around $50, so I decided to look at selling some $50 puts. The July $50 puts were around $1⁵/₈, the September $50 puts were at $4¹/₂. The stock was now firming a little in anticipation of the earnings coming out. It looked like a very good play.

I sold five contracts for the July $50 puts for $1⁵/₈ and sold five (5) contracts of the September $50 puts for $4¹/₂. I was a little hesitant to go out to September, but I asked myself, what's the worst that can happen? I would have to buy 500 shares of a stock I want at cost basis of $45¹/₂ in September (before its next earnings report). Sounds pretty good to me. (If this up trend continues as it has in the past, the stock could even split by then anyway.)

So today, Wednesday, July 10, Ascend closed up $3³/₄. The July $50 puts are now at ¹/₈ and the September $50 puts are now at $3. I collected a premium of over $3,000 by selling these puts, which is a lot cheaper than buying the stock outright and trying to realize a $3,000 gain. There is really not much downside risk here.

T.E.

THE STRATEGY

Okay, here we go. A stock is at $13.50. You really like the company. You think this stock could easily go to $18 or $20. You think this because:

1) The stock is rolling between $13 and $20, and has done so frequently. You know this from looking at its chart.

2) You have heard good news from the company—i.e., new products, expansion, great earnings, etc.

You could buy the stock or buy the $12.50, $15 or even $17.50 call options. If the stock rises as expected, the value of your investments increases. Both of these choices require an expenditure of money. If you buy the stock on margin, you only have to put up a percentage of the money (in most cases 50%). I bring this up here because margin requirements will be necessary when selling puts—see the section on "cash requirements."

Let's not buy the stock or call options. Let's sell a $15 put, or even the $12.50 put, if you think the stock may go down further. What does this mean? Let's use the $15 put example first. If you sell a $15 put, you are literally committing yourself to buy the stock at $15. You no longer have just the right (as in buying an option), you now have the obligation to perform, if the stock gets "put to you."

You see, by writing a put (selling), you have given some-one the right to sell you the stock at $15. They don't know who you are—all they have done is purchase a put option—giving them the right, not the obligation, to sell the stock to someone at $15. When would they do this? When the stock is below $15. Now, if the stock is at $14.75 or $14.875 on the expiration date, it's iffy whether or not it will get put to you.

(See "Selling Calls" in the *Wall Street Money Machine* for more information on the execution of these close orders.) However, if the stock is at $14 or $13 *it will get put to you* at $15.

What did you get for selling the put? And when will you get the cash? The premium you receive is determined by how far the strike price is in the money or out of the money, and how long until it expires.

> *PC Docs Group International (DOCSG) closed at $16¹/₄ today. This appears to be a stock that will return to its normal roll between $18 and $21 prior to August 12th. Moreover, the August $17¹/₂ put price is quite favorable. Even if you were called to purchase the stock at $17¹/₂ it would be a wholesale purchase which could be turned around at a profit in a relatively short time.*
>
> *I am an avid fan of W.I.N. and can't read Mr. Cook's book enough times.*
>
> M.F.—*Baton Rouge, Louisiana*

$15 PUT PLAY

If the stock is $13.50, you get at least $1.50 for the $15 put because that's how much the stock is in the money. Let's say you sell ten contracts. That will generate $1,500. However, that is all intrinsic value. Depending on the time to expi-

Stock Price	Strike Price	Option Price
$12.50	$15	$3.50
13.00	15	2.75
13.50	15	2.00
14.00	15	1.25
15.00	15	0.75
15.50	15	0.25
16.00	15	0.125
17.00	15	No bid

ration, there will be added to this the time value, perhaps another 50¢. That's $2 or $2,000. The cash will be in your account the next trading day. You now are obligated to purchase 1,000 shares of this stock at $15. I'll discuss movement and what we have accomplished, but to do so we need to see the relationship between the stock and put option prices.

Obviously, these prices are a snapshot in time. The option prices would be significantly higher if we went out several months, and significantly lower if the stock is not close to $15, or if it's just a few days until the expiration date.

Back to the strategy. Again, we have obligated ourselves to buy this stock at $15. We have made $2,000 cash and it is in our account. We now play the waiting game. The big question is this: Are we willing to buy the stock at $15, or do we want to buy the stock at all? If the answer is no, then you probably should not have sold the right to someone to sell it to you at $15. Simply put—you had better like this company, AND LIKE IT AT THAT PARTICULAR PRICE, or you should not have done this.

Okay, you have $2,000 cash in your account, now what do you want to happen? If you don't really want to buy the stock (which is my desire in about 99% of the cases where I've sold puts), but wouldn't mind, then you hope the stock goes up.

If the stock moves above $15 (or close to $15), the stock won't get put to you and you get to keep the money ($2,000). Remember, that was a deciding factor—you thought this stock was going up.

If the stock doesn't perform this way, then you will now own the stock. It will be in your account, the Thursday after the third Friday of the expiration month. Before we explore briefly what you can do with the stock, let's look at what happened.

BUYING WHOLESALE

You just purchased this stock for $13. You see, your cost basis is adjusted by the premiums you've received for selling the put. If you've ever wanted to buy wholesale, you've done so. You've taken in $2 for selling the put and now your $15 purchase price is adjusted by this amount and you have a $13 cost basis. Just think, this stock could be selling at $14.50. You could take the stock and sell it immediately and have a $1,500 profit. You could also:

1) Hold onto the stock for awhile. Remember, you thought this stock was going up. Is the story line still true?

2) Sell a covered call on all or part of the stock. You could now sell a call option at a $12.50 or $15 strike price, or wait for the stock to strengthen and sell the $15 call option for more money (hoping to get called out or not) or even the $17.50 strike price if it moves up a lot.

3) Go short on the stock, so you don't have to actually purchase it. I'll explain this later.

One thing I learned from my real estate days is that if you buy wholesale, all kinds of good choices present themselves. You can sell immediately and your payments are lower so you can rent at a profit, etc. The same is true with stocks. You have good choices if you buy wholesale.

OTHER BUY-BACK STRATEGIES

Long before we purchase the stock, and along the way as it is rising, there are still other things we can do to take advantage of the "magnified movement" in the option price. Review the previous diagram (page 74).

As the stock rises and gets close to the $15 strike price, the value of the put goes down. If it's awhile before the expiration date and the option is going for 50¢, we could buy it back. What does this mean? We buy a $15 put for 50¢. Now we have the right to sell the stock at $15. The option costs $500 for ten contracts (plus commissions). You're now creating a "wash" situation. You sold 10 puts, now you've just bought 10 puts and to your broker's computer it's a wash. They both go off the screen. You now have no obligation to perform.

You would only buy back the puts if there is plenty of time before the expiration date for the stock to go back down. If the stock is near $15 and climbing, or above $15 with a small chance for a significant decrease, don't buy the put. Just wait for the option to expire and you get to keep the whole $2,000. Your profit, if you buy back the $15 put for 50¢ ($500 for ten contracts) is $1,500. Don't unnecessarily spend money you don't have to. However, let's keep going. What if there is still plenty of time before the expiration date and the stock has shown a lot of volatility? It's at $15.50, the put options are 25¢, you spend $250 to buy them back. You have a clear profit of $1,750, minus commissions. Now, the stock falls back to $14. At this time the $15 puts are going for $1.25. You sell another ten put contracts and generate $1,250, then one of the following happens.

1) The stock stays down. Your basis is now $12 ($15 minus $3: $2 for the original put sold, minus 25¢ for

the put buy-back, plus $1.25; the selling of the second $15 put). That is a super wholesale price.

2) The stock rises above $15. You get to keep the premiums and you have no further obligation.

3) If there is still time to buy back the put again, try it again – repeat the process. Note: I've done two puts, but never three in one month. It's possible, but highly unlikely. The stock would have to be really volatile, having a lot of quick movement. Look at the following charts and plays:

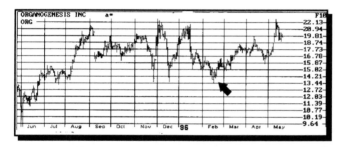

We sold puts at $15 and the stock went way up. We also had calls on this play.

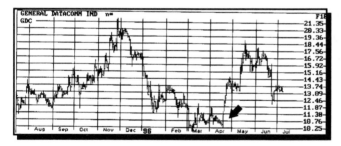

A good covered call stock can also be a good one for selling puts. We sold the $10 puts, then the stock hit $19. Profit $1,000.

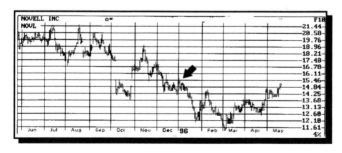

We sold the $15 puts. We actually got the stock put to us, but I like this company and don't mind owning the stock.

DUCks

Some of you have read elsewhere about DUCks—or Dipping Undervalued Calls. This is when a company, usually after a split, that has been climbing, pulls back temporarily as investors take their profits. The company is solid and growing, but the stock dips 5-10% for no reason other than profit taking. Around our office, we have a word for this. We call it a "SALE." The price of the stock and also of the options, has just dropped below value. It is a perfect buy opportunity.

Obviously, any buy opportunity or any rising stock also presents a great opportunity to sell a put. If the stock turns and rises (as it should) you keep the premium and that's it.

Of course, you want to pick the stock near the bottom of the dip and sell the put for the very next expiration date. And the strike price should be very near the stock price.

That way, if you're wrong and the stock gets put to you (you are required to buy it), you get it at the sale price where it can rise. And when you buy a rising stock, you can easily sell later at a profit, sell calls, or just hold it. So a DUCk really presents a great opportunity to enhance your cash flow.

GOING SHORT

Up until now we have been discussing selling uncovered puts. We don't have a position in the underlying stock (as in writing covered calls). If you wanted to sell covered puts, you could, now or later, sell short the stock. You could generate cash, ride the stock on down, and when the stock falls in price (which is your risk in selling puts) you could cover your position by being short on the stock. If the stock gets put to you, it will cover (end) your short position.

Remember, you've agreed to buy stock you don't own. Now you've borrowed stock you don't own—you're covered. Sounds crazy, doesn't it?

Think of it this way. If you have to purchase the stock at $15, and your broker immediately sells 1,000 shares in a short sale, your obligation is covered. Now if there is a dip in the stock price, the stock you buy (at this lower wholesale price) will cover your short position.

This is a hedge. Now, let's double hedge. You hedge a short sale by purchasing call options. If the stock is at $13 and you still think there will be an increase, buy a $15 call option. Now you have the right to buy the stock at $15. The risk of short selling is an increase in the stock price. With the $15 call options, you've purchased insurance.

If the last several paragraphs frustrate you, read them again, discuss them with your broker, and don't worry too much. I've sold dozens and dozens of puts. I've only had to do short sales a couple of times. If you do your homework, and then sell the puts when the stock is way down and rising, you won't have to worry about this.

CASH REQUIREMENTS

The only true hang-up to selling puts is that your broker will require cash on hand (in the money market part of your account) to cover your obligation. If you have a margin account, you'll need to have around 30% of the amount needed to fulfill your obligation. If the stock is at $15, that's between $3,000 and $5,000. The money market account will earn interest. If you have a lot of money in your account, they will be a little more lenient. They just want to make sure you can take care of your obligation to purchase the shares if you have to buy them.

The margin requirements for selling puts is actually 20%. Your broker will also hold the put premiums you've received (until the expiration date) minus any out-of-the-money amount. It will come out around 25% to 35%. Other factors figure in, too. How many other stocks and options you own. How strong is your relationship? Each broker is different. Yes, they have strict SEC rules to follow, but they have their own concerns. The primary one being this: what is the exposure if there's a major market downturn—say 30%? Can you purchase all you've requested to purchase, or is their neck on the line too? They will err on the side of caution.

PROFIT AT SELLING PUTS
Damage Control

You can't say that you have unlimited risk in selling puts because the lowest the stock can go is to zero. That is your downside. If the stock is below the strike price, it will get put to you.

You have one other strategy that can be played right up to and through the expiration date. It is called "rolling out." Here's the way it works. Let's say the stock is at $46. Last month you sold the $50 put for $2.25 when the stock was at $48.50. You had hopes it would go up. It hasn't. If you have to buy the stock, your basis will be $47.75, as you have received $2.25. One problem is the heavy duty amount of cash you'll need to purchase the stock—even $25,000 on margin.

You think you could find a better use for the money. The put is currently $4.25—buy it back. Actually, you're just purchasing the same put (strike price, month) as you sold. This will close the position—it's a wash on your broker's computer. If you had ten contracts, you would have lost a little over $2,000 after you add up the commissions. You could just end it here, but don't. There's another play.

Remember, you liked this company's stock at this price. Check it out. Is the story line still in place? Yes, it didn't go above the $50 like you planned—at least, not yet. If you still think it will do so, roll on out to the next month.

Let's continue. Try to catch the stock on a dip—even if in a roll or slam in trading. Say it's going between $46^5/$_8$ and $46^3/$_4$. It occasionally drops to $46^2/$_8$. At that point sell the November $50 put. It's going for $4.50. That's $4,500. You're back in the money again, and you've made a profit.

If you don't think it will go above $4.50, look at the $45 put. It's going for $2^1/$_8$, or $2.125. If you sold this you'd about break even on the original loss. Yes, you have an open position to buy the stock at $45, but your homework says it will go up.

Another method would be to split the contracts. Say, sell five of the $50 puts and five of the $45 puts. You should and could consider purchasing $45 or $50 calls. Maybe the $45's for November, and the $50's for February.

It keeps going down. Believe me, there will be an end to this—you will eventually make money. The next month the stock is at $44. Let's stick with the $50 puts as that will be most drastic. You sold the November 50 puts for $4.25. It will cost $6.50 to buy them back. This purchase will throw you back in the loss column. Not by much, though.

You're sure, this time, that the stock will turn around. It just has to (or so you hope). So spend the money—$6,500. Now the

December $50 puts are going for $8 and the $45's are going for $2. Sell the $45 puts. You're profitable again. Also, look at the $40's—there might be some premiums there.

Now the stock moves back up to $47. Your December $45 put expires worthless , and you've made over $2,000 for all this trouble.

This could go on several months—but sometime (hopefully) the stock will turn around. When it does, you end it and keep the best batch of each. When you buy back this month's put, you can always sell the next month out for more money.

AND FINALLY

There are two more considerations.

1) You may want to consider only selling, or at least primarily selling out-of-the-money puts, i.e. you sell the $50 put when the stock is at $52. This gives you a cushion. The problem is that the premiums are smaller and you have to weigh out the amount of margin tied up for the smaller option premium.

2) Stick with stocks in the $5 to $25 range. Selling puts and writing calls have a lot of the same risk/reward features—only in reverse. If you want nice premiums on stocks which won't kill you to buy, the lower priced stocks may work better.

Remember, when you sell you have many ways of making money (see "Tandem Plays"). When you buy call options or put options you only have one. This rolling out strategy lets you stay in the game until you make money.

It's simple: you generate cash whether you have to perform or not. If you do have to buy the stock, you purchased it at a less expensive price than otherwise. I love selling puts because you get the best of both worlds—cash now and wholesale prices.

11

OPTION EXIT STRATEGIES ON STOCK SPLITS

Many of my current strategies and much of my current profits are from trading options on companies announcing stock splits. Exit strategies shown here are as varied as entrance strategies. It would be appropriate to give additional sell plays and do so in conjunction with the whole play (buy, hold, sell).

GETTING IN—GETTING OUT
A) PRE-ANNOUNCEMENT:

I've had a lot of luck guessing which stocks are going to split. Except for Mobil Oil (MOB) (which may still split), I'm batting a great average. I look at several things to see if the company may be ready to split.

1) Do they have a history of splits— and how recent are they? *Value Line* charts have information on splits. Other sources can be used.

2) Price range. Companies seem to split when they get near or above their previous high. Currently, I look for companies between $60 and $150.

3) Profitability. Are they making money? Do they have growing revenues?

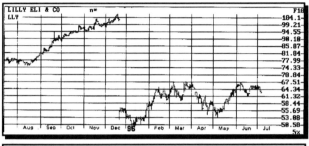

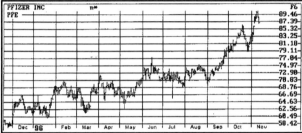

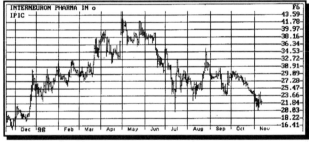

4) Dividends. Companies which pay dividends and announce larger dividends are good candidates for an increase in value. Companies which initiate dividends and do stock splits are great candidates.

5) Sympathy Moves. When other similar companies make stock split announcements, the hot potato passes on and can spread through a whole sector. Note LillyEli and Company (LLY), Pfizer Pharmaceuticals (PFE), Interneuron (IPIC) in 1995 and 1996.

6) Companies that have stocks which run up in value in the previous six months—more specifically stocks with almost a 90% angle. Look at the following charts:

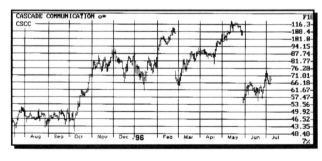

Cascade Communications (CSCC) stock in February of 1996, in the $105 range and again in May 1996. I'm going to continue to keep my eye on this chart.

Microsoft (MSFT) has run up nearly $40 in six months. This company looks like a prime candidate for a stock split. Again, I'm going to keep watching closely.

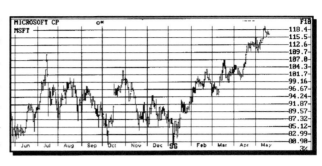

U.S. Robotics (USRX) split their stock back in September of 1995 in the $150 range, then again in May of 1996 in the $170 range. If this stock gets up around $160 a split is probably imminent.

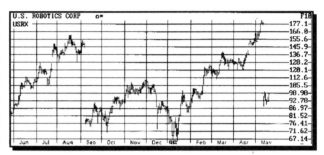

Iomega (IOMG) is one of my favorites. This company usually splits its stock in the $50 to $60 range. It is currently on another upward move.

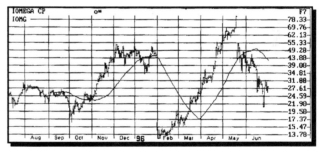

Cambridge Technology (CATP): This stock doubled in price in ten months, then they split their stock. It is currently on the rise.

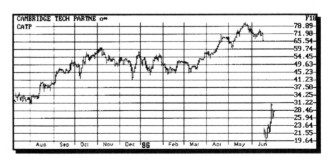

169

7) Find out when the board of directors meets, or when the annual shareholders' meeting is scheduled.

8) Check the information to be voted on at the shareholders' meeting and see if there is to be an authorization of new shares. Usually, but not always, this means a split is imminent (sometimes at the same meeting). For an example, observe Monsanto (MTC) in May of 1996.

Note: The directors usually don't need shareholder approval to do a stock split. However, they do need shareholder approval for new authorization of stocks because the shareholders numerical position will be diluted, hence the need for a vote. Check out Microsoft (MSFT) in the spring of 1994. They voted on more shares of stock. Shortly thereafter, they announced a 2:1 split scheduled to take place on May 23. Similar situations occur all the time, i.e. McDonalds (MCD) in May, 1996. Monsanto (MTC), voted on 140 million shares of additional authorized stock, then almost immediately announced a 5:1 split.

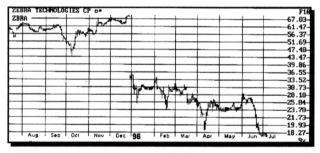

I played another one called Zebra Technologies (ZBRA) that took almost six months, but it was still a good play.

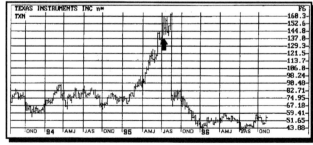

The one that got my attention was Texas Instruments (TXN). It was near $140. I'm not making this up, but at

12:30 P.M.. (PST–the stock market closes at 1:00 P.M.. Pacific Time), I bought some $140 calls for the next month, and a few $145 calls two months out. At 1:15 P.M.., fifteen minutes after the market closed the company announced a 2:1 split. They also increased their dividend. The stock shot up to $152 in the next few days and I got out at a huge profit.

> *You can't get lucky*
> *if you're not in the game.*

> *If you know exactly why you got in you should*
> *be able to choose the appropriate sell point.*

Intuition? Maybe. Luck? Somewhat. But I do it all the time.

B) AFTER THE ANNOUNCEMENT

There is stock movement upon a stock split announcement and, for several days thereafter, there is usually a lot of volatility.

1) The period of time around the stock split—the day before, the day of and the day after—has a lot of price fluctuations, usually positive in nature. Obviously, unless you pre-guess a split the day before it is announced, it comes and goes and you know nothing. Watch for quick run-ups, large volumes, etc.—something is usually afoot.

> *On May 8th, during my second Wall Street Workshop (in San Diego), I bought 10 Cognos June $60 calls at $1^1/8 on announcement of a split. On May*

171

14th, I sold them all at $16³/₄ for a profit of $6,927 and a return of 75.1%.

R.L.— San Diego, California

The day of the announcement is a good time to play, which brings us to #2.

2) The day, actually the minute of the announcements, is one of my favorites. The problem is getting instantaneous information. If you have a news service or a broker with one (and one who will call you), and more specifically if he can do a word search on the word "split," then you can move quickly. Sometimes, the stock moves up $2 to $3 in a minute. Your $4 can become $6 in seconds. No joke, in seconds. We love having a stock split announcement occurring during one of our live Wall Street Workshops. The attendees are amazed at how fast the options go up (and down). I do a lot of these as one day—even one to two hour plays.

3) A day or so after the announcement. If there has been a huge increase there is a tendency for the stock (and therefore the option) to come back down. That's why I:

   A) Sell almost immediately—even if I lose some potential profits – and get out at a profit.

   B) Wait to see a better trend or better support. If the stock doesn't go up at first, I hold back and wait. This gives me time to really think about it, and wait for more news, earnings reports, dividends, etc.

4) On volatility: if the stock has been volatile before the split announcement (check out USRX and IOM), then it will probably continue to be volatile after the announce-

ment and even after the actual stock split. If the company is a slow plodder—it will prob- ably con- tinue to be so. The play is to buy on dips and sell at peaks. Re-

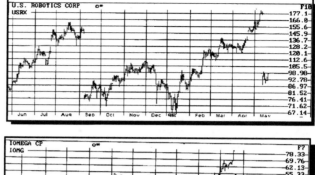

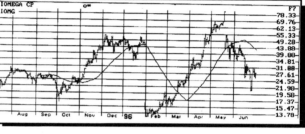

member: Don't worry if you miss the first move. Be happy.

5) Before the actual split. Usually, the stock splits about four weeks after the announcement. Sometimes, it's 6 to 10 weeks. Sometimes one week. Just before the split it may be a sale candidate. I've seen a lot of nice price increases during the short period before the actual split (exdividend date) and the day of the split. Then many stocks dip down. For example: an $80 stock runs up to $90 from the time of the announcement to the split date. The day before the split, it goes up to $92. It splits to two shares at $46. By the end of the day it's $47 and then a few days later it falls either to $44 or an $88 pre-split price. I've run across too many charts which show this pattern.

173

John Deere and Co. (DE) ran up almost $5 in one day, and continued to slowly climb for 2-3 days before it split. After the split, it immediately ran up $2-$3 and then slowly continued its upward trend for nearly one month before it backed off.

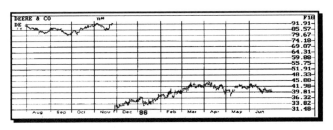

Pairgain Technologies (PAIR) went from the $100 range to $118 in a matter of days just before it split. Once it split, it gained another $4 before it dropped back down.

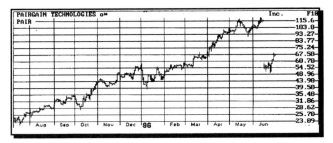

Bed, Bath and Beyond (BBBY) went from the $45 range up to around $60, one and a half weeks before its split. Post split, it continued to climb steadily for one month.

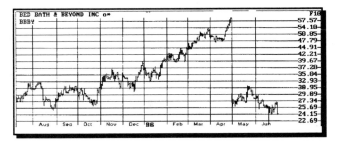

Computer Associates (CA) split its stock in the $65 range in September of 1995. At the time this chapter was being writ-

ten, CA was in split range again. I am going to watch this one closely.

Synopsys (SNPS) peaked up around $7 in the four days before it split. It peaked one day, and then gradually backed off a little.

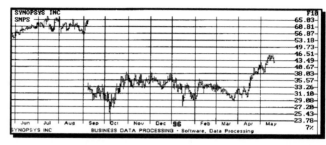

Phycor Inc. (PHYC) split in September of 1995, and again in June of 1996. Look at this chart. The trend was the same right after the split. This one is predictable.

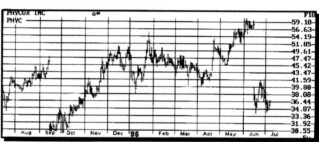

Iomega (IOM): Another one of my favorites. This was a very volatile stock before and after the split. I play this one often.

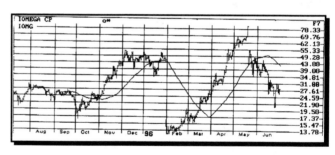

U.S. Robotics (USRX) is another favorite. Like Iomega, this is a very volatile stock. They split their stock two times in a nine month period.

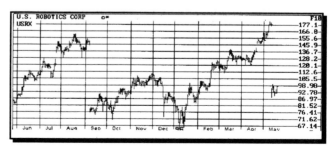

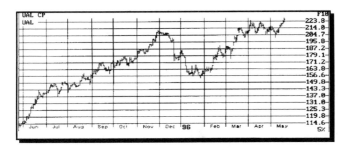

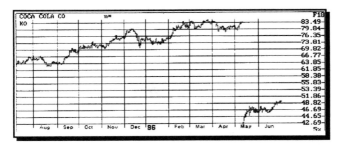

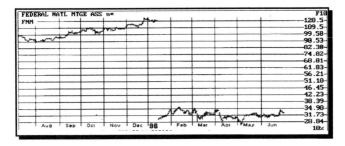

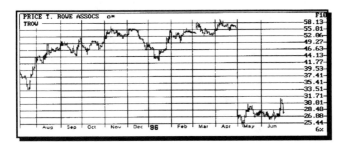

(UAL): Another favorite. I played this stock many times. UAL stock was at $220 when it split. Post-split it lost a little ground. We are still watching this stock.

Coca-Cola (KO) took quite a run up three days before it split. Then after it split, it ran up another $4 in the first week.

Fannie Mae (FNM) is one I play a lot. This stock stayed steady for about six months before it finally split. The steady trend is the same as post split.

T. Rowe Price (TROW) had already reached its split range in November, 1995. They waited until May to split their stock.

It will be interesting to see what happens if TROW reaches $55 again.

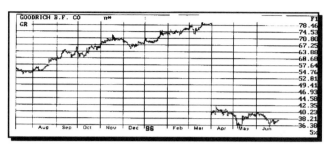

B.F. Goodrich (GR) climbed steadily to an $80 high over the course of nine months, then they split their stock. Now, it is running between $35 and $40 every month.

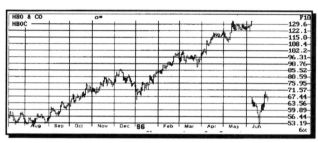

H.B.O. and Company (HBOC) took a nice steady run up to the $130 range. After its split in June of 1996, it went down a little, but is recovering nicely.

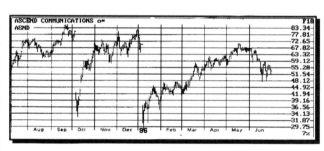

Ascend Communications (ASND): Look at this chart. This stock has played out a mirror image of itself every time it split.

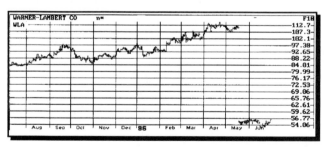

Warner-Lambert (WLA), McGraw-Hill (MHP), and Chubb (CB) are typi-

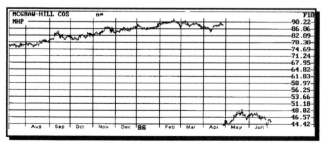

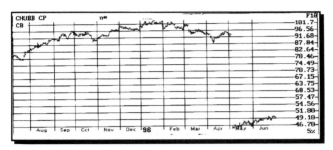

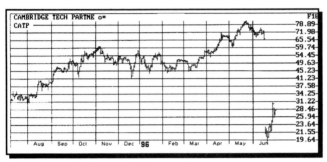

cal of high priced stocks. They show very stable trends and predictibility. These will probably continue to rise at a slow, steady pace. This shows stability and strength in a company. I like to see charts like these.

Cambridge Technology (CATP) ran up on the split announcement, then backed off a little. After the stock split, it had an incredible run upward before it leveled off. This one is worth watching.

I can hardly ever find a stock that breaks this trend. I guess the quick pop-up cannot be sustained and it weakens once reality sets in. Investors start really examining it. (What is the stock really worth?) The euphoria is over; new news comes out, like lower projected earnings or similar news.

I bought two contracts of Coca-Cola's (KO) August 80 calls after reading about the split announcement on W.I.N. I paid $6³/₈. Coke took a dump so I bought two August $75 contracts on April 11 for $7⁵/₈. Anyway, on the August 80's I made $525 on a $1,275 investment in 64 days= 41% return=239% annual return. August 75's, I made $1,525 on a $1,525 investment in 35 days=100% re-

turn=1,042% annual return. All of this was before I attended the Wall Street Workshop, which I attended in Sacramento last week.

Jim—Sacramento, California

Also, here's a quick observation I've made. The stock (during and just after the split) moves, as do a lot of stocks, in sympathy with the market in general.

What does all this mean? If you're profitable you may want to exit just before (a day or hours) or just after the actual split. There will always be more time to buy back in. Yes, you might lose some potential profits, but this is more often the case: You purchase an option for $4, the stock was at $81. You own the $85 call. The company announced the split on June 2, and it is to take place July 5. You own the August 19 expiration date options. You've done it right. On July 8, the stock is at $87 and your option is $6, a nice 50% profit. On July 18, the stock shoots up to $90 and your option is worth $8—a double. On the 20th, the stock is at $46 ($92 pre split) and your option is now $5.25. Should you sell or wait for it to go up more? On the 22nd, the stock dips $4 to $42 and your option (now the August $40 call) is $3. You are still profitable, but a lot less so. What if it dips further?

In this case, I would have sold. (I'm not just conjecturing here. I mean, not only would I have, I did sell at $5 or so.) I do this all the time. My people on W.I.N. wonder why I sell so quickly and so often?

Think about it. Wouldn't it be better to sell at $5.50, wait for a dip (even if it takes weeks or months) and buy back in at $3 (for the August) or even $4 for the September options? If the stock doesn't go down and there is more good news—if there is still plenty of time – buy back in at the September or October $45's or $50's.

RANGE RIDERS

The road back up may take years and it definitely will not be a straight-shot freeway. Look at the following charts:

Worldcom (WCOM): This stock shows a nice steady upward climb, and at last report was still going.

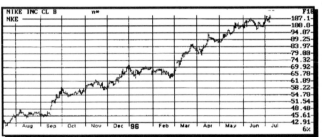

Nike (NKE) is another good example. It has steadily made its way to the $105 range over the last year. I like this stock.

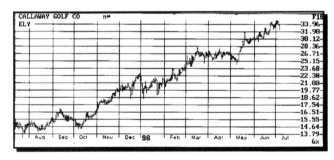

Callaway Golf (ELY): Again, a typical climb to the top. Stocks as predictable as these can be very profitable.

Northern Telecom (NT) has gradually climbed from $35 to $55 in nine months. This chart shows a nice steady climb upward with plenty of rolls.

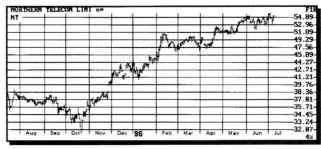

You can get in and out many times along the way. You can buy the stock and wait it out, or you can buy the stock and sell. Proxy investing with options allows for a greater return and many short-term profits. You have less cash tied up and you can jack up your profits by being nimble and quick.

12

TANDEM PLAYS

This chapter is about winning—and winning big. No time for mediocrity and no time for second best. My continued drive as an educator is to consistently find new, better, faster ways to make money. I love a barbecue (BBQ). To me it stands for Bigger, Better, Quicker Returns. In dealing in the stock market this means returns, yields—money back in. In short, more INcome—INfaster, INbigger quantities, and INmore often.

I'm not alone in this endeavor. My students countrywide share ideas, hints, techniques that have helped them make more. I've become a clearinghouse of ideas—some boring, some not too hot, but many are great ways to enhance our earning potential. For years, I've said I want to help people get their money working as hard as they work. Now, after nearly two decades as an educator, I realize why people had a quizzical look when I said that. They actually want their money to work <u>harder</u> than they do. I also realize one other thing: you've all heard the one about working smarter, not harder; well the real-life application of that is to improve upon those investors who are "true doers," who really think about what they're doing—who can and do improve upon their methods, their results, and their applications.

If you like to deal in stock options, these new ideas—actually variations of how we look at and use old ideas, will help you see new avenues, fortify your resolve for perpetual and consistent income, and actually help you generate more cash flow.

This is a tough order for some of you, because you're doing so well. Others need this information to get off dead center. Maybe by explaining option alternatives this will be accomplished.

However, no matter who you are or why you're reading this, you should have read other reports or books (hopefully written by Yours Truly) on option investing. You should be familiar with calls and puts. If not, stop now and go back to the basics.

WIN MORE THAN YOU LOSE

I've repeatedly said that two things make stock market investing profitable:

1) Be right more than you are wrong.

2) Be willing and able to act quickly. If you haven't figured out by now that options move extremely fast and big when the underlying stock moves even a little, then there may be no hope for you. It's not this aspect that I want to deal with. It's the first point—being right more often—that I'll write about. You've heard the one about Babe Ruth striking out more than 3,000 times on his way to the home run record, so I won't

bring it up here. And even if I did, that's only part of the point I'm about to make. I want to help you stack the deck in your favor.

So, after all this set up, let me just say the main point—the theme of this chapter. Then I will explore it, dissect it and put it to work.

Here it is:

> **"When you sell calls or sell puts you have a two out of three chance of making money."**

The deck is stacked in your favor. I'll follow up with diagrams and explanations, but first let's look at the four plays.

All of these deal with options, a derivative based on an underlying stock. I like stock options because they are not a pure gamble (as are index options, currency options and interest rate options) and you actually can buy or sell the underlying stock.

Let's quickly review the basics. A call option is the right to buy a stock. You can buy call options and you can sell call options. A put option is the right to sell a stock. You can buy put options and you can sell put options.

Buy	Stock Price	Sell
Call	Rises	Call
	Steady	
Put	Falls	Put

Look at the diagram closely because we're going to explore variations of these options.

185

Let's explain this further and then see how you win two out of three times—and maybe every time if you do it right.

WHY AND WHEN
Buying Calls

You buy calls (short and long term) when you think a stock (hence the option value) will increase within a certain time period. You do so to lock in a certain price for the stock or to sell the option at a higher price. Your risk is that the stock (option) won't increase in value in the time allowed.

Selling Calls

You sell calls to generate income. When you sell a call, you are committed to perform. You've given someone the right to buy stock from you, whether you own (covered) the stock or not (uncovered, naked). The premium you receive adjusts the basis you pay (paid) for the stock. For example, if you bought a stock at $9 and sold the $10 strike price call for $1 and then had the stock bought from you at $10, your profit would be $2. Your basis is $8, as the $1 premium reduces your basis from $9 to $8.

You can systematically generate monthly income from writing (selling) calls. You sell naked call options when stocks are high and you expect them to go down or stay the same. (See the chapters on covered calls in the **Wall Street Money Machine**.)

*I have what I feel is a great "buying put" story. Following in the great tradition of Wade Cook's **Wall Street Money Machine**, I purchased 20 contracts of* *a put on LSI Logic Corp. (LSI) at $2^{13}/_{16}$ on July 2, at a $25 strike with an October expiration date. I also did a call strategy on this stock as well.*

This stock then became fairly stagnant and I almost sold my put yesterday (July 9) for not much profit, but I held on one more day and on Wednesday, July 10th, I was able to sell my put for $4^5/_8$. This gives me a profit of approximately $3,625.

T. H.—Kentucky

Again, you can write covered calls and uncovered calls. If you write uncovered calls you qualify the investment for an infinite rate of return, as you have no cash tied up. You also have an added risk in that you may have to purchase the stock for resale if the stock rises above the strike price and you get called out. Obviously, this risk is mitigated by the premium you've received. For example: If you've sold a call (when the stock was at $11) for a $2 premium at a $10 strike price, you'd hope for the stock to go below $10. You'd only sell the call if you thought the stock would go, or stay, under the strike price, so you could keep the premium with no further obligation. For other variations, attend the Wall Street Workshop.

I nearly paid for the cost of the course with three days of investing! I know you at Wade Cook Seminars will believe it, but I'm sure others will not. Thanks for the best business course I have ever taken. I highly recommend the Wall Street Workshop to anyone who is interested in financial stability. Sounds crazy to accomplish this in stocks. Just test it! Knowledge is the key to the stock market. Thank you for providing the information I needed.

R. T.—Anaheim, California

I really like to sell uncovered calls. It takes experience and more cash in your account to do these, but it's fun and very profitable.

Buying Puts

Now, let's get on to puts. The right (option) to sell a stock to someone increases in value as the stock moves downward and away from the strike price. If the stock is $38 and you think it will go down, you could buy a put option with a $30, $35, $40 or $45 strike price. The one you choose depends on:

1) How far down you think the stock will go.

2) How much you want to risk (your option premium).

3) How much time before the expiration date.

4) Other important factors: a) whether the stock rolls between certain ranges, b) news regarding debt, mergers, new (good, bad) management, etc.

A $2.50 premium to buy a $40 put will increase in value as the stock moves to $36, $35 and lower. You can sell or exercise the option any time before the expiration date.

Selling Puts

If you sell a put, everything turns upside down. You are selling the right to someone to put the stock to you at the strike price. Why do this?

1) To generate immediate income. Think of it. If the stock goes above the strike price you won't get it put to you and you get to keep all of the premium.

2) You buy the stock wholesale. Let's say the stock is at $13 and you sell the $15 put for $2.50, the stock

doesn't rise above $15 (maybe it is $14.50) and you get it put to you, your basis is $12.50. You've just bought a $14.50 stock for $12.50.

When do you do this?

1) When you want to own stock in a company, or, at least, you wouldn't mind owning it.

2) When you wouldn't mind owning it at that price— and wholesale, to boot.

3) YOU WANT TO GENERATE INCOME—NOW!!

CROSSOVER

Now that we've established the four plays, look at the following diagram.

You see, there are three things which can happen to the stock (and we assume this movement will affect the option price to a certain degree): it can stay the same, or about the same, it can go up, and it can go down. However, if you sell a call or a put, a lot of opportunities open up. You

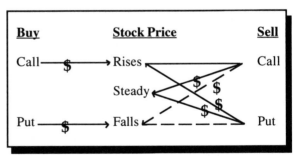

should see here that you could sell a put in the situation where you normally would think of buying the call (you think the stock is going to rise) and sell a call when you would buy a put (you think the stock will fall). The difference and the key point is that when you sell something you generate income.

The dotted line means that you would also "sort of" make money as the stock price falls, in that the premium received would lower the basis paid for the stock.

So, if you think a stock is going up, you can sell a put rather than buying a call to put dollars into your account instead of spending it. That's cash flow: selling rather than buying. If you 1) buy back the option you sold at a lower price, or 2) let the option expire, you get an infinite rate of return. By selling options, two out of the three possible scenarios (stock rises, stock stays steady, or stock falls) are profitable. When you buy options the stock must move one way. Only one profitable scenario exists. Look at the following examples:

Naked Calls

The stock is, say $9, and you write the $10 call and receive $1.50 premium. If the stock rises above the strike price and you are called out, you keep the premium, but you have to deliver the stock.

If the stock stays steady at $9 or falls below $9, you can either buy back the call at a lower price when the time value decays, or you could wait for the option to expire. In either case, you would receive an infinite rate of return.

Naked Puts

The stock is, say $11, and you write the $10 put and a $1.50 premium. If the stock stays the same or rises, you keep the premium and you can either buy back the put at a lower premium or wait for the option to expire. Either way, you get an infinite rate of return.

If the stock falls below the strike price of $10, you have the stock put to you. You would have to accept the stock at $10.

Covered Calls

If you purchased the stock at $9 and wrote the $10 call for $1.50, you would receive a $1.50 premium. If the stock rises above the strike price ($10), you would be called out, and you would keep $1.50 premium plus make $1 on the sale of the stock.

If the stock stays steady, you would not be called out. You would keep your $1.50 premium and you could write more calls the next month.

If the stock falls, you keep the $1.50 premium which can offset the loss on your stock. Then you have to make a choice, do you wait for expiration or buy back the call at a reduced price? You can find more information in *The Next STEP* and the *Wall Street Money Machine*.

Covered Puts

Covered puts are an odd concept to explain. In a covered call, you own the stock, so you can deliver it if the option is exercised against you. In a covered put, you have to have a place in your portfolio prepared and ready to accept stock if it is put to you, i.e. you must have a short sale position in that stock. This is a very advanced strategy that we cover in detail at *The Next STEP Wall Street Workshop*.

> *I like selling puts on a stock that I would like to own in a long-term position even through market turmoil. By selling a pricey put, you can take advantage of the speed of options and, if it all goes well, you can buy it back at a profit. If it doesn't all go as planned and it gets put to you, you will just own a stock you wanted anyway. You can start selling covered calls at the strike price you paid (after adjusting for the premium collected) for the stock when the stock has regained strength before a dip. Then, when*

it dips, you buy the call back. Continue to sell these perhaps deep-in-the-money calls until you get called out.

I have been doing this with Ascend Communications (ASND). It seems to work well because it is such a great stock for this strategy. This strategy could be disaster for someone who tried this with Micron Technology (MU) a while back. Perhaps buying some cheap puts at the same time may work as a safety hedge. Options can be risky this year. I find that buying options when the McClellan Oscillator is in an oversold condition can help me not get stung by a correction or market rotation. Keeping track of future event dates like jobs reports can be helpful, too. The bad thing is that one can wait a long time between these safer trading periods. A strong, long-term, up-trending stock can make a big difference.

A.L.—LaMirada, California

STOCK LOW—GOING UP

Stock Price	Put Price ($15.00)	Call Price ($15.00)
$13.00	$2.50	.25
13.50	1.75	.50
14.00	1.25	1.00
14.50	0.50	1.25
14.75	0.25	1.50
15.50	0.125	1.75

Sell Put—Buy Call

If you sold the put for $2.50 ($2,500) and bought the call for 25¢ ($250), you would have a net in of $2,250. Now, as the stock increases, you can either buy back the put or just let

192

it expire (in most cases). The call could now be sold for $1.50 or $1.75, generating more income.

> **You get rich (cash flow rich) by selling—**
> **get better at getting out than at getting in.**

> **If you have to get in, do so at wholesale prices.**
> **If you have to get out, do so at retail prices.**

STOCK HIGH— COMING DOWN
Sell Call—Buy Put

Stock Price	Call Price	Put Price
$15.75	$1.50	.25
15.00	1.00	.75
14.50	.75	1.00
14.00	.50	1.25
13.50	.43	1.50
13.00	.125	2.25

Sell the call for $1.50 ($1,500 if you purchased ten contracts) buy the put for 25¢. Capitalize on each—depending on the time left before expiration—at the optimum time. Buy back the call or let it expire and sell the put at a profit.

> **You know I like getting rich in bite-sized pieces**
> **—Two plays on the same movement—**
> **talk about two mints in one!**

Once again, so many more opportunities open up when you sell than when you buy. Don't misunderstand; I still make most of my money buying calls—on pure option plays. I try, however, to sell as many calls and puts as I can.

Remember, writing covered calls is a great strategy for IRA's and other pension-type accounts.

Generating income, infinite returns, buying stock wholesale, double-dipping with highly volatile stocks (selling two calls or puts in one month)—are just so much fun.

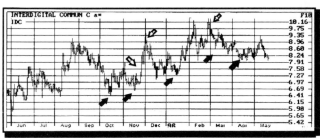

Now look at the following charts to see possibilities. I added arrows to show the buy and sell ranges.

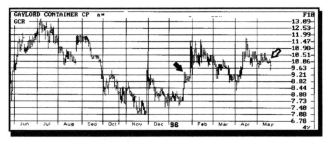

Opposite

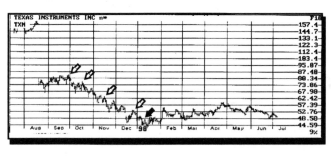

⬦ Buy a put, sell a call.

◆ Sell a put, buy a call.

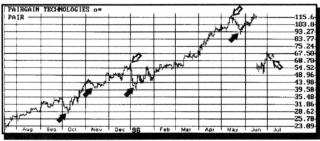

⬈ Buy a put, sell a call.

◣ Sell a put, buy a call.

Look at how many opportunities a volatile, but up-ward-trending stock options.

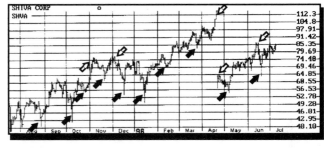

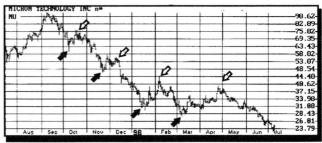

And on and on...

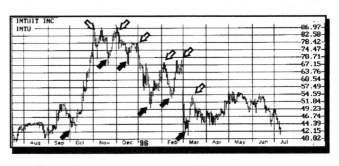

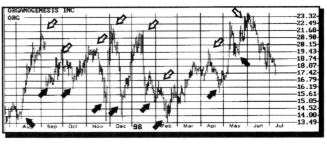

Read the following example: You find a stock that is rolling, rising from $13 and bouncing off $16. It's down to $13 and is rising quite rapidly. When it hits $13.50, you sell the $15 put for $2. Ten contracts equals $2,000. Nice cash flow.

Now, when the stock gets to $14.75, the put is going for 50¢. You buy it back at a cost of $500. You get to keep the $1,500 with no further obligation. However, why not cross over and sell the $15 call? Do this when the stock is at $15.50 or $15.75. Yes, it might rise or stay above $15 and you'd have to buy the option back at a small loss, but the $15 premium could easily be $1 to $1.50-another $1,500 of income. Remember, check the charts. This one is moving rapidly. It may go under $15 and you'll have a second premium—yours to keep. Now as it dips down and starts up, repeat the process.

True, when it's above $15 and you think it's going down you could do a pure $15 put purchase play. And yes, when it hits $12 or $13 you could do a pure $12.50 call or $15 call purchase play.

You could even do a double play.

1) Sell a $12.50 put and buy a call when the stock is at $13 when you believe it's on the way up. The premium will be about the same. However, as the stock rises, the money you received for selling the put looks better because the put value goes down (remember, you sold it when it was nice and high). At the same time your call premium goes up in value. Sell the call now for a profit and keep the profit for selling the put, or even buy back the put while it's low. Wow, I can't wait for the market to open tomorrow. And yes, we can wax philosophical all day long—hey, if I have to poten-

tially buy the stock at $15 and I've purchased the right to buy it at $15, what if it's close? Your brain might catch on fire.

2) Sell a call and buy a put when you think a stock may go down a bit. This way you pick up the nice call premium. If you own the stock, you won't get called out. The dip is offset by the rise in value of the put option premium. You can sell the put option at a profit.

If you don't own the stock, you keep the premium for selling the call and then get to sell the put at a higher price when the stock goes down. This is a form of hedging, and what a hedge it is!

Now, don't make this too complicated. You've read about rolling stocks and rolling options. You've heard me teach about peaks and valleys. You've heard of some straddles—buy a call and put on the same stock, same month, same strike prices, and wait for a big move either way. Well, I call this a side-straddle. A calculated, predictable way to capture the up movement, or the down movement—TWICE.

I cover this more extensively at **The Next STEP Wall Street Workshop**. You'd be smart to be there. Call 1-800-872-7411. These seminars sell out, so call now. Note: **The Next STEP Wall Street Workshop** is only available to **Wall Street Workshop** graduates, or people with more stock and option experience. Come to the "BBQ."

Appendix 1

Money Mysteries Of The Millionaires

The following is an edited transcript from one of a series of cassette tapes by Wade Cook, entitled Money Mysteries of the Millionaires.

Hello, this is Wade Cook. This is going to be a totally different tape than you've ever listened to before in your life: Mysteries of the millionaires, especially in regard to money and finances. I've got to give you a little bit of background about me in case you have not listened to any of my other tapes or read my books.

I was a cab driver in Tacoma, Washington. I got involved in real estate by going to other people's seminars. I tried it. I tried the old rental game. I didn't have any money to get started, so I borrowed money from my father, ended up with a bunch of rental properties and I wasn't making any money. I ended up selling a property, carried back a mortgage on it, then I started thinking, "Man, I stumbled onto something here. This is great." And I started making all kinds of money by selling properties, not by buying them. So I'd buy, I'd fix up, and I'd sell and usually, I'd carry back paper. Not always—sometimes I got cash, but I'd usually carry back the paper on the property, and I had all these monthly checks coming in. Those monthly checks allowed me to retire at the early age of 29. Now, I've been out for the last two decades, teaching people how to get rich buying and selling real estate, using stock market strategies, and more. I'm going to talk about many of those strategies here. But, a lot of those strategies are included in other cassettes that I've done, so I'm not going to talk about the money *making* things here so much as what rich people do to get wealthy and to stay wealthy.

I'm going to go through a list of five points, and along the way I'm going to shed a lot of light on some other minor points. I think that you'll see some different ideas here, and maybe an idea that you haven't thought of.

Now, I wish I didn't have to say this next thing because there are so many people out there who think that the way to get rich is to have a goal or to have a plan. It's as if all those goals set you up for failure. Goals cause you to get discouraged and quit. Now, don't get me wrong. I'm really big into priorities. I'm really big into directions, into targets, and I like that, but typical goal setting just hasn't worked. People say, "Well, get control of your time. Get control of your life. Have a goal. Have a plan."

Well, everyone, throw all that garbage away. Wealth comes from chaos. You find me any rich person, any rich company that's ever been organized. Now, don't get me wrong: you can organize the chaos later on, but at the very beginning, you have to do something totally wild, totally different. You have to stick out. You have to be crazy. (I mean, I eat Chinese food almost every morning for breakfast just to remind myself to be a little bit strange all day long.) You have to be chaotic, and out of this chaos, then, will come a lot of good things that will happen to build up a fortune for you.

The second thing that rich people are not afraid of is failure. I mean, they literally are risking failure a lot of times, usually not with their whole estate, but with a lot of money. They're not afraid of failure. The opposite side of the coin of failure is success and if you're willing to risk failure, you can have all kinds of success.

Most people have come to the realization that they can make a lot of money. But, to do so, they need to make their money in bite-sized pieces. You know, back in the early 1900's, the Wright Brothers changed the history of the world with that short flight in Kitty Hawk, North Carolina. That flight changed everything. But, do you know that from the point where that little Wright Brothers' plane took off to the point where it landed could be flown inside of a Boeing 747? I mean, you need to think big, but you need to think big in a whole bunch of bite-sized pieces.

Now, how do these all mesh together? I kind of feel like I did when I wrote my book called, *The Real Estate Money Machine*. I've written fourteen books since that time, showing people how to make money and how to keep and preserve their wealth. I feel a lot like Thomas Edison when he was trying to invent the light bulb. He needed that little filament to go across there. He tried, perhaps 1,000 different items to go across there. Nothing worked. Finally, by accident, he stumbled across Tungsten and it worked. Somebody said, "Well, how did you make this all work?" And he said, "I failed my way to success." You know, I feel the same way. I tried real estate. It wasn't working good enough for me. I ended up as a fluke and everybody told me I was crazy. I ended up selling my property. Well, it worked! I mean, I had all this money coming in from this property, and I did it again and again and again. See, the bottom line key to wealth is duplication and repetition; it's a hamburger in Tampa Bay which tastes exactly like a hamburger in San Francisco Bay.

That is the key to wealth. To find something that you can duplicate. So, in my real estate, I was able to duplicate it because I put the emphasis on selling. I kept recycling the down payments and made a whole bunch of money. Now, I've done my *Money Machine* seminars, my Financial Clinics all around the country showing people how to do that. I used to try to keep track of all the people who retired. I mean, look, I'm in the retirement business. I don't just teach people how to go out and make $5,000 or $10,000 on a house. I try to show them a system, a track to run on, that will make them tons of money, and I used to try to keep track. I used to have file drawers full of people that have been successful that had retired. I can't even keep track anymore. There's just too many around the country. But it's a phenomenal way, if you put the emphasis more on getting out of something than getting into something.

Now think about this, because this is a lesson I learned from one of my attorneys—and by the way, most attorneys give you such bad advice, this is some good advice that I got from one of my attorneys. She said, "Don't ever go in the entrance until you know the exit." Boy, what good advice that is. Don't ever buy a house unless you know exactly what you're going to sell it for. Or, possibly, have it sold before you ever buy it. Don't ever buy a stock unless you know what you're going to get out of it. Now, I do have some stocks that I hold, but when I'm doing my rolling stock thing, I'm buying and selling and I do so within a certain range. I know what I want to sell that stock for before I ever get in.

All right. Another thing that rich people are good at, number three, is that they get good at making effective decisions. They're not afraid to make decisions. They're not afraid to take the risk as we said, and risk the success and failure, but they're also not afraid. They're good at making effective decisions which means this: they're really good at gathering up information, and the better you get at gathering information (when the gathering time stops) then it's time to think and to ponder and meditate about the decision. You can do such a better job, and then when that process is over with and you actually decide to do something or to not do something, the implementation of what you're going to do is so much better.

Now, let me say this another way: the better you are at gathering information, the better you're going to be at implementation. Conversely, the worse you are at gathering information, the worse you're going to be at the implementation. So, they're really, really good at that. Now, let me tell you a concept that I have that maybe you can use to help you make some decisions. And, I'm going to do this in regards to my Cook University.

Several years ago, I wanted to come up with a program that literally would change the way adult education is handled in this country. Now, I cannot change the way Americans think, but I can sure change the way several Americans learn and go about that for adults who are willing to get involved and really want a good results-oriented program. Now, let me tell you, I was considering computer programs. I was considering all kinds of tutorial manuals, you know, read this and go here and go here, and I could not come up with something that was really different and unique until this.

One day, just out of the blue, kind of when my brain was down and I wasn't even thinking about it, I started thinking, "Wade, what did you need? What did you need back when you first got started when you were sitting there staring at a house?" And the answer was, "I needed someone who had been there before." I needed a mentor. I needed somebody who had done several hundred deals and would say, "Hey, write up the offer this way. Don't get involved in this one. Buy this one. Do this." Somebody to show me, not just tell me how to do it, but to show me and someone to watch over my shoulder; watch over me while I was doing it. Then, I got involved in a whole bunch of bad apartment buildings in Detroit, and I started losing my shirt and it rippled through my whole net worth. I mean, I had these bad deals. I had to sell off all kinds of my good investments to pay for the bad ones. What did I need at that time? Again, the answer came. I needed someone who had been there before. And then, when I started making really good money, started paying taxes, I mean, hundreds of thousands of dollars a year, what I started thinking about was the same thing. What did I need? Well, I needed somebody who'd show me, who could show me how to structure myself, someone who had been there before. And not some CPA making $35,000 a year who's never had to make payroll, not some attorney who makes $50,000 - $60,000 a year who's never had to really buckle down and to pay those kinds of taxes, but somebody who's really been there before. So, what I came up with, the outgrowth of all this was Cook University, and I've been doing it for several years.

I've taken 30, 40 classes of people to boot camps and through Cook University, and the results are phenomenal. I mean, it has been the most detailed-oriented, functional results-oriented program I've ever put together. It involves a mentor program about which I'm going to tell you as we get down to number five, but I'm trying to prove a point right now about making effective decisions. See, later on in this tape, you're going to be able to, you're going to turn this tape off and we'll never talk again. Some of you are going to decide to come to the program and once you say, "Yes," to that, then a whole bunch of new possibilities open up. But, if you say, "No," then you're left to your own devices, and we'll talk about that in just a minute. But, if you say, "Yes," then you come on and you come to the training and you get the support.

Now, what I'm talking about, everyone, that I want you to get involved in here on this tape is a process that I have called "Projected Hindsight." Now, we all know that hindsight is 20/20. I want you to think about this: projected hindsight. Let me tell you what it means. A few years ago, my daughter was 13 and I had adopted her when she was 7. When I married my wife, she had two daughters. They were 7 and 4 at the time and I adopted them about a year after we got married. And I love those two girls, and we've had three kids of our own since that time. And, I've been their dad now for the last dozen, you know, 13, 14 years. But when my daughter was 13, she came home from junior high school one day and she said, "Dad, all the girls at school are wearing makeup." Now, she was 12$^1/_2$, almost 13. "Can I wear makeup?"

I said, "No." Now, I don't want to impose my standards on you, but I cannot see any good from a 12 year old girl wearing makeup. And I said, "No, you can't, but you know, when you're 13, you can start wearing it every Monday to practice, so when you're 14, you can start wearing it regularily." And that's just that. That was the rule at my house. Boy, she was upset, but she's a good kid and she bought into it. She was okay.

Then, a couple of days later, she came home and said, "Dad, the kids are having a teen dance after school and I really want to go to this teen dance on Friday night."

Now, here she was, almost 13, beautiful blond haired girl, and I said, "Nope, you can't go. I'm sorry. You cannot go." Boy, now, there's weeping and wailing and gnashing of teeth because she really wanted to go to that dance and she's a cute girl, and she dances nicely. She really wanted to go. But, I could not think of any good that could come from her going to the dance—I can think of a lot of bad. Kind of reminds me of Bill Cosby and his book on fatherhood. He says, "Knowing what I know now about 14 year old boys, they should all be arrested and put in jail." Well, I kinda felt the same thing with my pretty daughter there, and I just didn't want her to be exposed to that.

Well, she didn't talk to me for a couple days, and I walked into her room after school one day, and I said, "Brenda, we need to talk. You know, you're almost 13 years old. You know, about ten years from right now, you're gonna come home one day after having a little baby. You'll hold this baby in your arms, your daughter or your son, and you're going to be looking at that baby, wondering what kind of a mother you're going to be. Are you going to be strict? Are you going to be lax? Are you going to spank the kid? Are you not? How are you gonna love 'em? What are you gonna do? And you're gonna come home one day and you're gonna say to me, "Dad, back when I was a teenager, I'm really glad that you let me do my own thing." I'm really glad that you didn't care about me. I'm really glad that you didn't care about my friends. I'm really glad that you didn't care about the grades that I got in school. By the way, she's not 23 yet, but hopefully, she will be saying, "Dad, I'm really glad that you were strict and you had rules and you enforced the rules. I'm glad that you let me hate you for awhile so I could kinda grow through that and I'm glad that you, you know, loved your family enough to do those kinds of things." Now, hopefully, what will she be saying? That is the process I have called "Projected Hindsight." You take a time, five years, ten years, whatever, and you project out and you say, "What is it that I want to have accomplished during this five or ten years?"

Now, I'm not going to let you off the hook here. Gotta come back and talk about financial things. If you are in your 50's, and by the way, your 50's should be a powerful time of your life. You can look at age 50 and say, "When I turn 60, what is it that I want to have said about my 50's?" And then you get on with it. And then you go out and do it. You see the process there? Now, if you use this process for helping you make decisions, then a lot of things will become clearer. For example, what I want to help people do, what I really get a kick out of, is helping people retire so that they can spend more time with their family and their friends and with their churches and do more. If I'm on a crusade at all, it's that I believe in something and that is: our kids need more help, and they need more constructive time with their parents. And the way our society is today with, a lot of times, two parents working, then we need to be able to come up with the kind of incomes that we get money working for us rather than us working for money and get the money producing income so that we can spend more time with our kids and our grandkids.

We are constantly being asked to make decisions with information that's not complete. See, a lot of people come up to me at my seminars or they want me to come look at properties with them and they'll say, well, "Mr. Cook, is buying this house a good deal? Is buying this fourplex a good deal?" And I say, "Well, I don't know. What else could you be doing with your time? What else could you be doing with your money?" See, that's the question everyone: "What else?" You don't ask, "Is this a good deal?" You say, "What else could I be doing with my time and money?" And then, hopefully, you'll be able to come up with the right kinds of answers. So, buying this house, might be right, or maybe a stock market investment may be better.

One time a guy came up to me at a seminar and had one semester to go. But I got him so excited at the seminar about doing my money machine, he wanted to quit college. I said, "No, just finish. Finish this, and, three months from now, four months from right now, you can go out and do all the real estate, but go ahead and get your degree. You're that close." You see, so it's a question, a trade-off. Everything in life is a trade-off. If you get involved in this stock, then you can't buy this stock. If you buy this house, you can't buy this duplex. Everything in life is a trade-off and you've got to have proper information so that your money gets working for you the best way that it can, which is the next point.

Point number four. (And by the way, "mystery," that's kind of a funny word because it sounds like something that is ambiguous, that's nebulous and nobody can ever under-stand. I treat real estate information, tax information, investment information, kind of like going to see a magician. You know, the first time you see him do a magic trick, you say, "Ooo, man! How did he do that?" But, if he were to show you how, you'd say, "Piece of cake, you know, anybody can do that.") Once you see wealthy people get rich, and you see what they do, the way they do it, then you know how they do it repeatedly.

Let me tell you a quick story. I was doing a seminar a few years back in Philadelphia, and it was like the middle of November. It was sleety, a little bit rainy and a little bit foggy, and it was just a horrible day. Not only did I have to give a seminar in Philadelphia, but it was north of Philadelphia in Jenkintown. I had 13 boxes of all my books to sell at the seminar. And I got up there and sure enough, there was the Hilton. I pulled around the corner and went through a bunch of trees and I pulled up in front of the hotel.

I got out of the car. I unloaded all the boxes. I was sweaty and a mess and it was horrible out. I went into the hotel and I could not find the name of the seminar on the marquee. So, I finally questioned around and they said, "I'm sorry, they, we just don't have that seminar here." By then I realized that I wasn't in the Hilton. I was in the Holiday Inn. I had pulled around the corner, pulled in the wrong parking lot, gone right past the Hilton and pulled into the wrong hotel. It was so foggy out, I could hardly even see the hotels anyway.

Well it was 10:30 in the morning, and I still had until about 2:00 in the afternoon, and I was tired. So I just walked down this hallway after talking to the banquet manager, and I noticed a woman in this room. I love seeing a good seminar and boy, she was good. I mean, she had these women up and down and doing all kinds of stuff and she was leading this little rally in this room—she was so good. I stuck around for about 45 minutes to talk to her afterwards.

Now, her name was Janet and she'd told her story that she was making about $12,000 a year many years before. Now, with this new company and this new sales promotional thing that she was involved in, she was going to make $60,000 this year. With the Christmas bonuses and all that coming up, if she did a really good job, she was going to make $70,000 or $75,000. Now, in two or three years, to go from $12,000 to $75,000 is phenomenal. And, by the way, the company was Mary Kay Cosmetics and she worked for them.

Now, the reason why I'm bringing all that up is because I want to ask you something. If you would take Janet out of that situation, stick her in any other company, any other sales type of thing, would she be a success again? I mean, once you learn how to be a success one time, can you be a success again? And the answer is, "Yes." Which just proves to me that most success characteristics are learned. People are not born with them.

You can literally watch what rich people are doing and just mimic that and copy that. For example, a big part of what I teach in my Wealth Academy seminars is how to structure corporations and how to set up these different entities so that you are maximizing your control. And, that you can make money. You can learn how to make all kinds of money, but then write it off and put it off to another company, put a bunch into a pension plan so that you've got all kinds of wealth that you're building up, but you're not sending it all off to the IRS. The point I'm trying to make, everyone, is that rich people learn how to be in control of their money to the point that they get money working for them.

There are two areas of control that I like to talk about. One is the area of asset control or entity control, and the other one is the area of taxes. Let's talk about assets for just a minute. Well, there are really six different legal entities that I think you need to get a handle on. I'm going to go through the list here very quickly. (If you need more information on this, I've got whole, major, all-day seminars on these, and I'd love to have you call our 800 number and get information. Get our whole catalog, get a listing of my books. Get a listing of my seminars coming into your area.

One entity is a corporation. I like the Nevada corporation. It's my preferable state of choice even more than Delaware. In Nevada, there's no corporate tax, no stock transfer tax, no franchise tax. There's no tax at all. In the state of Nevada, the officers, that means you, mom and dad, the president, vice-president, cannot be sued for the activities of the corporation. Nevada is a total secrecy state. Nobody can ever find out who owns the stock in your company and, by the way, you can even have bearer stock, and you can even have nominee officers and directors which means that your name doesn't have to be associated with the corporation at all. You can take your sister-in-law, who is on welfare, making $12,000 a year and have her be the officer. You're just a general manager and a signatory on the account. You're an employee of the company, but your name is not associated as the legal officer. And Nevada is the only state which has not signed an information sharing agreement with the IRS. There's no reciprocity. You know what that means, by the way? That means Nevada collects no information to share. So, the IRS cannot get access to their information. Now, this is why there's more corporations filed in Nevada than all the other 49 states put together. A big part of what my company does now is, we have offices in Las Vegas, we have offices near Seattle, Washington, and we set up Nevada corporations for people, literally hundreds of them a month. We give people structure so that they're making money but they're making it in a smaller tax bracket.

Now, that's when we get to taxes, I'll bring that up again. (Anyway, if you want to get some information on Nevada Corporations, or any of our entities, you can, again, call the same 800 number. It's 1-800-872-7411.) Now, let's continue to talk about controlling assets. Living Trusts is a necessity with our weird probate society today, I mean, probate is horrible. The cost of probate, the time of probate, the cost it takes to get through probate is a horrible expense. The only way to avoid probate is to not die. Now, the other way that is almost fool proof for avoiding probate is to have a Living Trust. See, you die as a pauper.

So, you set up a Living Trust. You put all your things into it: stock in your corporations, units in your limited partnerships, everything that you own, is assigned to the Living Trust. Your personal residence goes in there, and then upon death, when you die, there's no cause for probate because the judge doesn't have to transfer anything from one person to another. It's all handled in a Living Trust. Good living trusts are designed to avoid probate.

Now, some attorneys think Living Trusts are a panacea for everything. You take your rental properties, you take your business, and you take everything and stick it in Living Trusts. I say, no, no, no, no, no, you can't do that. If you have a rental property in a Living Trust and one of your renters sues, they can come after everything else in your Living Trust. You cannot do that. The Living Trust is designed to avoid probate. That's what it's for. If you have rental properties, those should either be owned in a corporate structure, or, my favorite would be a limited partnership for owning rental properties, because it's a great way to own a property and pass through the tax benefits.

Now, I'm going to talk about Limited Partnerships from another point of view also, and you know what? It's hard to talk about an entity without talking about the functionality of the entity and what it does. But, let me just pose one quick thing so that you get a handle on this. A Limited Partnership is an entity that you establish. It gets it's own federal ID number. It can be in business. It can have brokerage accounts. It can own stock in corporations. It can do anything that you are going to do, and you can do it just as well in a family Limited Partnership. The reason I say family is because usually it's only family members involved. Now, follow me through on this because the Limited Partnership is really quite remarkable.

You can divvy up the units in the partnership. A small percentage to mom and dad, a large percentage to each one of your three or four kids or your parents or whoever. Now, the partnership pays no taxes. There are no taxes paid at the partnership level. The partnership fills out a form 1065 at the end of the year for all of the unit holders, so, if your daughter, your eleven year old Karen, owns 11% of the units, then 11% of the profits or losses are going to be taxed down through to her. Now, by the way, your 11 year old gets no money. You don't write her a check. This is all allocated to her. It's a book entry, and you just pay your taxes. You take all the money home as the parent and you pay your bills and you pay the house payment, go to the movies, go do whatever you do. Your kids have this money allocated to them, and you, as the parents, are going to have to pay the taxes on that money.

But, think about this, if you have a little company making a hundred thousand dollars a year and you have it all divvied up among five or six or seven different people, then ultimately, all the money is going to be taxed at 15%. You see that? Instead of having a hundred thousand dollars, which is taxed at 15%, 25%, and some of at 31% to you, you now have a hundred thousand dollars out of your company and have it all taxed at 15%. Usually with your personal deductions and all that, this amount is offset almost down to zero for you as a husband and wife and maybe 15% on a few more of the people that you have who are supposedly taking money out, but aren't getting any of the money.

This is a Limited Partnership. Oh, by the way, let's say that you are worth a lot. You could take and give units to your kids or grandkids and you, as a general partner (by the way, your general partner should be your Nevada Corporation because then you avoid all personal liability) can be in full control of all this. So, even after you've given away a substantial amount, say 99% of all the units and the general partner still owns 1%, you're still in control. So, you're 60, 70, 80, 90 years old, and you've got millions of dollars, potentially, owned in three or four or five different Limited Partnerships or several different corporations.

You're in control. You get to draw out any kind of income you like. You get to put more money into pension plans, whatever you want to do, and you're in control. And then, over the years, you can gift off units or the stocks in your partnerships or corporations to your kids and your grandkids or your church or whoever else you want to ultimately have all these things upon your death, and it's just such a great way to go. Again, it's control without ownership. You don't want ownership. You want control.

Now, one more point on the Limited Partnership. Let's go back to our hundred thousand dollars that you're making as a family. Now, if you as the husband and wife receive, oh, I don't know, five or ten or fifteen thousand bucks for managing the partnership, or whatever, that money is earned income. You have to pay social security taxes on that. Let's take a little time out on social security taxes. How many believe that social security is a good deal? You know? Take it out of your pay check, putting money in social security. I mean, there are people out there that really believe it's a good deal! They think that if they turn 65 and haven't put money into social security they're not going to get anything back. Well, that may be true, but why would anybody ever want to put their money into social security?

See, if you could take the same money and earn four and five and six percent on it and have that compounding, you're going to get out of social security, at the age of 65, until you die, about 20% of what you put in or what it could have been. 80% of your stuff is just going to go up in thin air, not to you. By the way, when our congressmen start paying money into social security, then maybe I'll feel differently. Private pension plans, your own IRA's are such a better way to go. So, now think this one through. Social security is a bad place to put your money. Do you know that all that hundred thousand dollars that you just pulled out to the unit holders of your family Limited Partnership is unearned income?

You just pulled out a hundred thousand bucks of unearned income and there's no social security tax on unearned income. So, every investor in your little business just dropped out of the social security system. You can quit putting your money into such a wasteful government program. It's a phenomenal way to go.

Let me move on to number five. The number one thing that I see that almost all rich people do and all successful people do is to surround themselves with a team or have person as their mentor. They surround themselves with people that know more than they do and/or have talents and abilities and/or can see what they need. For example, I think Martina Navratalova is one of the greatest woman tennis players of all time, but every time before she went on the court, she met with her coach. Joan Sutherland, Beverly Sills, two of the greatest woman opera singers of all time, before they go on the stage, they practice for months before their voice teacher. Why? They're the best—they're the best in the world. Why do they need a voice teacher? I'm reminded of Albert Einstein. He was being honored at a New York banquet at the age of 75. A pretty young hostess for the evening took his arm and sat him down for the night and was sitting there beside him. They were up at the podium saying all these nice things about him. After about a half hour of this, she looked at him and she asked, "What is it you do, sir?" He looked back at her and he said, "I'm engaged in the study of physics." And she looked back at him and she said, "Oh, physics. I studied that last semester." Now, think about the difference in their answers. Here he is, the most renowned physicist in all the world, and he did not even say, "I'm a physicist." He said, "I'm engaged in the study of physics."

Now, everyone, from a financial point of view, that's what I believe I am engaged in: the study of finances, whether it's corporations or entity structuring. See, you've all heard of financial planning and you've all heard of estate planning. But I'll bet you haven't heard of entity planning. Well, that's what I do. And that's the niche that my company has found itself: we set up entities for people. We don't get into commissions. We don't sell any investments. We help people structure their entities so that they can keep more of what they're making. They can move money from one state to another. They can move money from one tax bracket to another. They can move money into a Charitable Remainder

Trust and get deductions right now and have some charity get the money 30 and 40 years down the road. That is what we do-the Corporations, the Living Trusts, the Charitable Remainder Trusts, Business Trusts, all phenomenal entities. If you have a business right now with equipment, did you know that you could set up a Business Trust with an equipment leasing operation and have income paid from the business over to the trust as renting the equipment? And, then if someone were to come in to sue you, they could never take your equipment away because you're just leasing it and there's a priority lien on the equipment from some other company? That's a Massachusetts Business Trust that does an excellent job of doing that strategy. The Family Limited Partnership, as I mentioned, and Corporate Pension Plans and Keogh Plans, that's what my company does. We help people set up their entities and we have major trainings on that part of it, not only on making money, but on the whole asset protection, tax reduction, liability reduction, bequeath-ment process.

See, everyone, when you go out into that ring of life and you've got your boxing gloves on, you're up against some pretty powerful people, attorneys, insurance companies, a lot of people who are willing to take away everything you have. I'm going to talk about the three things that can go wrong in life. There are three problems. One of those problems is a lawsuit, another one is income taxes, and another one is death taxes. These are the three financial giants. Now, think about those three things: Income taxes, lawsuits, and death taxes. If you make all the money that you're gonna make under you, and if all the income that you have is made under you and if all your assets are held under you, then you stand pretty vulnerable. One lawsuit then wipes out everything. One income tax bracket for every-thing. You see, and the answer to all three of these is to split up your assets to make sure that you do not own all of your things in one legal entity, especially, by the way, in Joint Tenancy. Now, I personally believe joint tenancy should be outlawed in this country. I think it's that dangerous, especially between a husband and wife. It's one of the worst ways you can own anything. You should own things in a Living Trust. Then you should own your investments in your businesses and other entities, what we call sponge entities. If something goes wrong with something, they'll suck in anything that can go wrong, but they do not let it back out to contaminate anything else. For example, the corporation or the limited partnership.

So, the three entities that you use for being in business are the Corporation, the Limited Partnership, and the Business Trust. The entity that you have that kind of controls everything to avoid probate and then to make sure that things go to a stepped up basis is the Living trust. If one of the spouses wants to sell off their house or their investments, they can do so without paying capital gains because a Living Trust establishes a new, what is called, a stepped up basis. Why not make money and get wealthy in an entity that pays no taxes, like an IRA. More specifically, you can put aside huge amounts of money into a corporate pension plan and even borrow that money. You can get leverage to work so that you do not have to work so hard. And, I'll show you how to do that on some of our more extensive seminars.

Everyone, I am convinced that most people out there do not make it because, well, because they haven't learned how to make it. They don't deserve to be rich. Now, what are you doing to deserve to be rich? I can show you what you can do to deserve to be rich, and it really comes down to knowledge and information. I see that there's this huge amount of wealth on the other side of this chasm, this gap, and here's you on this other side, and you're looking across and you're saying that I know that all that wealth exists over there, but how am I going to get there? And, by the way, I'm going to ask you right now, what have you tried? Read some books? Everyone, I love books. I write books. I hope you read my books, but if books made people rich, librarians would be the richest people in the world. See? What have you tried? Investing in stock market? Oil? Gas? What have you tried and why hasn't it worked? The only thing that consistently works is this, and think about this because everything that you have learned how to do and to do well, you were hand trained by someone else.

You did not learn how to drive a car by reading a manual. You learned how to drive by getting behind the wheel and having somebody else say, "Okay, now push in this. Go here. Turn this. Do this. Do that." You had somebody show you how to do it. And probably before you started driving the car, you watched that person extensively to see what they were doing. Then you think you had it figured out when you finally got behind the wheel. Somebody could tell you, then show you, and watch over you while you're doing it and that's what works. Why should things financial be any different? You think that by going to a simple seminar for a few hours it's going to make you wealthy? It usually doesn't. Then why is there a difference? And I even see that in my courses. People who buy my set of books and tapes, and I've got really great sets of home study courses. Some people take that information and go home and are just incredibly successful. Other people do nothing. What is it? Now, I've watched this for many, many years. I've been doing seminars for almost two decades, writing books and all that. I've been wondering, why do some people make it and some people don't make it? Well, everyone, I can count the success stories on a few fingers of people who have just read my books. The people that get all my home study courses with forms and documents and apply the material well, I got hundreds of those. People who have come through my extensive training? I've got thousands upon thousands of those that have actually gone out and been successful. Why? Because they are willing to invest time and money. They are willing to come and learn and tie into a mentor consultation program where they can become an apprentice, you know, an apprenticemillionaire.

Now, think about that, an apprentice multimillionaire. A lot of people come through my training that are already millionaires, but they're scared. They're afraid of a lawsuit. They're afraid that their money's not making them a lot. They want to make sure that their family gets everything. And they're getting such bad advice from their CPA's and their attorneys who do not know how to structure people. Again, everyone, it's what I call entity planning, and I hope that we can spend some time together. In short, everyone, your families are too important. Your retirements are too close. Your assets are too vulnerable to leave this up to chance. You need to come and get this information. I'll be happy to have my staff go over all the pricing, the tuition, daily schedules, and get you the information that you need. Come and experience this most remarkable program. So, call 1-800-872-7411 and ask about the whole Cook University program, especially our flagship course, the Wealth Academy. Thanks for spending time with me. This has been Wade Cook.

You can make money or you can make excuses, but you can't make both.

A W.I.N.dow Into Wade's World

The following are excerpts from the June 1996 through November 1996 Wealth Information Network (W.I.N.) daily messages. W.I.N. is a network managed by Wade Cook and his team of financial instructors solely for the benefit of you, his customers. If you would like more information about W.I.N., or would like to join the service, please call 1-800-872-7411.

I want to try and explain what my stockbroker is trying to teach me on my morning sessions riding to and from my basketball game. He uses a lot of technical analysis—stochastic and moving averages. He mentioned Accustaff (ASTF) today as a possible quick turnaround play. I looked at the June options and I may jump in and buy some, but the only thing we have are options that traded last Wednesday and Thursday. So, I couldn't get a fix on what they will be trading at this morning (I was checking on these before the market opened). As of this taping, the market is not open. What my stockbroker is saying is when stocks or options move against the averages then it will have a tendency to correct itself. Both, historically and statistically. He uses a 14 day moving average which basically says that if the stock moves three deviation points away from the average it will probably correct itself. I questioned him on these deviation moves and how big they have to be and how they figure those. He said he could show me on a chart, if I could get to his office, but he couldn't readily explain it over the phone. I do want to get a little more technical, but not too technical. I am so busy making money, sometimes the technical analysis part of this may drag a person down. You could get so involved in trying to figure things out, you never make any money. You spend all your time trying to figure things out. I am not big into that, but I am big into figuring out how to jump in at the opportune moment. That's my main objective right now and questioning the stochastic and the technical analysis behind this. If any of you have help on this, please send me an E-mail (addressed to SYSOP). I have just purchased several books on technical analysis and I will be studying them. I started to studying them, but I was reading the paragraph five or six times just trying to understand it. I just don't see this cab driver being very good at understanding a lot of the technical things. But, what I do understand and can re-explain to you I will make my best stab at it.

Hello everyone. McDonnell Douglas (MD) 2:1 split is reflected today. The stock is around $50. This stock climbed up from $90 to over $100 before the split. The stock was up $^1/_8$ just a few minutes ago. I own a lot of the July $95 calls options. They are in the same price range where I bought them, so if I didn't have any I would buy them again. I also have my order in to sell my June $95 calls (which are now June $47.50 calls) at $5.

I played Cambridge Technologies (CATP). The stock is around $74.5. It looks like it is at a good low from where it has been. It has been in the low $80 range. Right now the stochastic chart (which measures the momentum of the stock) looks like it could bounce. It is coming up a 3:1 stock split June 19. When this stock announced the split it was around $47 to $50. I put in my order to purchase five contracts of the July $70 calls and they were trading around $8.75 x $9.25.

Iomega (IOMG) is trading around $40.675 x $40.875. The June $45 calls are trading around $2.125 x $3. That is $5 out-of-the-money. So, if you were called out, in addition to the $3 premium, you would still make another $4 or so, which would make the return (if you were called out) substantial. You run the numbers and see what you think.

IMP, Inc. (IMPX) is trading around $13.50 x $13.25. The June $15 calls are trading around 75¢ x $1. The premium is not as nice, but it is one of those companies that mirror Iomega (IOMG). It would be a 7% return or a 25% return if you are called out.

I want to report on a nice little rolling stock and one of my old favorites: Cineplex Odeon (CPX). I purchased some shares a few weeks ago at $1.50 and I bought a lot a long time ago at $1.375. I already sold some at $1.87 and it is now around $2 x $2.175. I am going to wait for it to strengthen just a little bit more and hopefully, I will be able to sell it at $2.25 or $2.5 before it falls back down.

There is quite a bit of action on rolling stocks right now, but they are just going a little too slow for me. I see more and faster action in the options. Remember, you can do the rolling stock strategy on options. It is a little more expensive, but a lot of them you can do with around $500. When I put in an order to buy 10,000 shares of stock at 20¢ that's only $2,000 if my order is filled. So, it is a small mount of money that I am working with repeatedly.

Good morning everyone. This could be a very interesting day in the market. This is one of those crazy days where everybody thinks the market will be slammed, and it probably will. The unemployment reports are out, and they are not bad, actually they are quite good. More jobs have been created, but unemployment went up 0.20 of 1% up to 5.6 %. But, because it is so good and the economy is so good, they are figuring the Federal Reserve will step in and raise interest rates which will drive the bond market down and the stock market will follow. Go figure this kind of reasoning. It happens almost every quarter, but it is totally crazy.

Medic Computer system (MCSY) announced a 2:1 stock split this morning. The pay date is July 9. The stock is trading around $86.50. Their earnings are $143 million and I don't know if that is gross or net, it has 11,000,000 shares outstanding, and it doesn't seem to be very widely traded. In mid-May, the stock was around $99 and it is now to the $86 range. Between November and February it was trading between $58 and $65 and since February it has run up to $99. The options hardly have any trading going on, and I don't want to buy a lot of these if I am not going to be able to sell them. I checked on the July $85 calls, the July $90 calls, the August $85 calls and the August $90 calls and there is barely any activity. I put in my order to purchase two contracts of the July $85 calls and the two contracts of August $90 calls. I did that in two different accounts, so if my order is hit I will have four contracts each. My stock broker made the comment after reading my book, that according to my terminology this stock looks like a range rider in its lower range.

Remember Imal (IIML)? It did a 4:1 stock split and it was not a typical split. It was a merger and anybody who had 100 shares ended up with 400 shares of stock in a new company. The stock is currently trading around $9 or $10 and I bought this stock at $21. If I sold it right now, it would be like selling it for $36 a share, so I placed my orders to sell.

With ComAir (COMR) I have the June $23.375 calls and the June $26.675 calls. I bought the June $23.375 calls at $1.30 and they are currently trading around $1.31. I bought the June

$26.675 calls at $2.84 and they are currently trading around $3.875 x $4.25. Remember, it is an odd strike price because of the 3:2 stock split. They give you more shares per contract. You have the same number of contracts, but now it is 150 shares per contract.

I don't know if this is exciting to you or not, but it is to me—Dayton Hudson (DH) announced a 3:1 stock split as reported earlier on WIN. I purchased the October $105 calls at $11.125 and they are now trading around $10.125 x $10.875. I am not certain of the pay date yet and the stock is down a little. This still should turn out to be a nice play, since it is 3:1 stock split. I decided to put in my order to purchase the July $105 calls, which are trading around $6.50 x $7 and the July $110 calls, which are trading around $4.125 x $4.50. I placed my order for ten contracts on each one of those options.

Iomega (IOMG) is trading around $41.25 x $41.50 and has moved up. There was news out that NEC is going to bundle their zip drive with some of their package. The July $45 calls were trading around $5 x $5.375. The July $50 calls were trading around $3.375 x $3.50. These are in the 20% range and if you were called out it would be an incredible return—but for the stout of heart only!

I will look at IPO's for a week or two out and try to get lined up to purchase them. They are very hard to get involved with and there are only so many shares on the first go around. But, some of the specialists at different brokerage firms are really into them. I want to play this marketplace to a certain extent. I have made money in the past on them. If any of you know of companies that are getting ready to do any kind of an offering, please e-mail us and let us know.

I did get hit on US Robotics (USRX) yesterday, I bought the June and July $85 calls. The stock went up and I should have probably gotten out at even $1 profit, but I was trying to get $2. The stock is now down $2 under what it was yesterday. I just checked a little while ago and the stock was around $87.50. I checked on the July $85 calls they were at $8.75 x $8.825, and the July $90 calls were at $6.825. This was a few minutes ago, and this stock is very volatile so you want to check on this one yourself. I think I am going to wait to see if it weakens a little bit more. I did not want to buy the July $85 calls, because the term is really short. I told my stockbroker to go ahead and buy me five contracts around $7 or $7.50 if it gets down that low.

Cellular Technology (CTSC). They have announced a 2:1 stock split and I do not know the pay date. The stock was around $40 last week and it bled down to around $36.50 on Friday. It looks like it could tick up about 75¢ this morning. I don't know what will happen to the options and I don't know for certain what will happen with the stock. One of my brokers, who does a lot of charting, claims this stock is at the bottom of the channel and looks good right now. I don't have any prices yet, but I will be looking at the July and August $35 calls and $40 calls. I will report exactly what I get after I finish playing basketball. I did tell my broker if it looked good to go ahead and get me involved and purchase 10 or 20 contracts.

For bottom fishing purposes, I am looking at some Russian stocks: Luke Oil, Monsenergo and Unified Energy. I will report more on them later. I have not made a big foray into foreign stocks, but I think there may be some plays here. This is after reading about 20 different companies. These are the three I have selected.

I also looked at JLG Industries (JLGI) once again, and the stock was down under $70. When this company made its stock split announcement about month ago the stock shot up over $80. I am going to go ahead and do a squeeze play with just a little bit of money. I am not going to buy very many contracts of the June $65 calls. The calls were around $8 about an hour ago. I put in an order to buy the calls for around $7.50, but the stockbroker held it back and waited for it to weaken, so I bought them for $6.50. Hoping that this stock has bottomed out, I am going to try to sell them at $9 or $10. I want to caution you not to do this kind of play unless you have a stout heart. I only played two contracts at $6.50, which comes out to around $1,300 with commission.

Last Friday we went into Cambridge Technology (CATP). While it was down, we thought it was doing a dead cat bounce, so we bought into some June $70 calls. It was up this morning a little bit, but now it is moving back off. We are probably past the point where we would have see a good bounce for profitability. We are now going to crawl out of those, even though we will be taking a little bit of a loss. It is better to do this and keep the capital to work with rather than lose on it. We did order back out at market his morning and I am waiting for confirmation on those orders.

I told my stockbrokers that I wanted to play a dead cat bounce on a lot of these. So if the stock was at $50, I wanted to play the July $50 calls or the July $55 calls, and hope for an up tick in the stock. I gave them marching instructions on about six different stocks, and told them to do their best. However, hardly any plays had gone off, because so many of them had already bounced back up. Some had bounced up $1 or $2 and already pulled back $1. The point that I am trying to make is that when a stock gets slammed one day, you have a couple of choices. One would be buying the option or stock at the end of the day if you think it is going to come back up. The other choice would be to get it right at market open, but sometimes if the stock has gone down to $26 like Iomega (IOMG) did, and it opens at $29 or $30, it is pretty tough to get *involved in a bounce because the bounce is already taken out of the stock almost before the market opens. If you are looking for a one or two hour play, you have to get in and get out right away. I am trying to teach the strategy because as far as I know, I did not get involved in any options plays this morning, because they just ran up too fast.*

I did a covered call play on C-Cube Microsystems (CUBE). Most of you know that I don't like doing covered calls when the stock is around $25 to $30, but this stock was at $33.75 and I bought 300 shares of the stock and then sold three contracts of the July $35 calls for around $3.

Hi everyone. I am standing in front of the class at our Wall Street Workshop in Bellevue, WA. I just heard that Eurotech (EURO) is up in the $9.50 range. I have 6,000 shares and I put my order in to sell them all at the market. I hope to get $9.50. I purchased these shares up between $5.825 and $6.125. Not a bad play for two weeks! I also put in an order to buy back 5,000 shares of Eurotech (EURO) at $7.

On February 2, 1996 Wade bought 1,000 shares of Lone Star Hospitality (LSHO) at $3.75, because it had announced a 3:2 split. On April 25, 1996 he decided to sell 1,000 shares at $4.75. Due to the 3:2 split Wade still had 500 shares in his account. What happened between then and now is that the 500 shares of Lone Star Hospitallity (LSHO) turned into 250 shares of Citdel Computers (NOFF), because the name of the company changed. It also did a 1:2 reverse stock split. Remember, when a stock does a reverse split you have 0.50 as many shares that are worth twice as much. He then sold 250 shares yesterday at $12.375. Wade doubled his money on this play.

Good morning. Wade's broker just phoned in with a 2:1 stock split announcement. The company is PHH Corporation (PHH).

Standard & Poors gives them an A- rating and they have a very positive outlook. The stock is trading around $55.25 x $57 (big spread) and there are no options available. PHH Corporation (PHH) is a vehicle and real estate management company. Be sure you do your own research and know your risk factor before purchasing any stock.

I looked at the Chrysler (C) August $60 calls. They are trading around $5.50, so I put in my order to purchase ten contracts. The August $65 calls are trading around $2.375, so I put my order in for ten contracts of those too. The stock is down $1.50 and I put my order in to purchase 20 contracts of stock. Remember, this stock is coming up on a stock split.

I also have some American Oncology (AORI) left over after I was called out in one of my pension accounts. I was going to sell the July $22.50 calls. I put my order in to sell two cotracts at $1.50, because I only have 200 shares left. My broker wasn't quite sure whether I had the stock in my account or not. This is an interesting thing, and it happens quite often, but often it takes a day or two after the expiration date to find out what you really have in your account.

With JLG Industries (JLGI), Wade is playing a dead cat bounce. It has dipped to as low as $67.75. While Wade was on the phone with his broker the stock went to $68.75 x $69.75. It looked like it was moving so Wade put in his order to purchase ten contracts of the July $65 calls at $8.50. He also placed an order for five contracts of the August $65 calls at $12.125.

Wade also did a covered call play on Orthologic (OLGC). They just did a 2:1 stock split and the stock is trading around $10.25 x $10.375. Wade placed an order to buy ten contracts and wrote the July $12.50 calls. This is an OTS order, which is an Order to Sell at $1.25. On top of that, Wade is also selling 20 contracts of *the July $15 calls for around 0.50. He is going naked (not covered with stock) on these 20 contracts.*

As always, do your homework, check with your broker, and know your risk factor before purchasing any stock or option. Remember, when you sell puts you are agreeing to buy the stock at a certain price. Iomega (IOMG) got up pretty high, so I looked at buying the July $30 put options which were around $3.50. This was pretty high, so I decided, instead, to sell them right now and then buy them back. If I did get the stock put to me, I would be buying at $26.375 which I am willing to do. I sold 10 contracts of the July $30 puts on Iomega (IOMG). The July $25 puts were $1.75. I sold 10 contracts of these also. If I did get them put to me with these options, I would be buying the stock at $23.25. I would say this is a good wholesale price compared to where the stock is right now. I must admit that I am amazed that the put premiums of the $25 were so high. The stock was $5 above the strike price and it still was a really high premium.

Good morning everyone. It is a few minutes before the stock market opens. I have a feeling that this is going to be a slow week, with July 4th this week, so I am not gambling on too many robust plays. With the lack of volume in the market, there will probably be a lot less up movement. After speaking with several of my brokers, I think there is some consensus that the market will be having a summer lull right now. I don't know the cause of this, but for the first time in a long time the market is feeling weak. So, I guess the word is just caution and I would not gamble on any big plays. Obviously, there are always winners among the losers and even with the market going down there are still some good plays that can be made. But, overall, one of the lessons I have learned is not to fight the trend. Do not swim upstream when everybody else is swimming downstream.

I will be very cautious in the next few weeks and try to buy options on weakness and take advantage of the negativism in the market. Here's an example: Coca Cola (KO) is around $48 to $49 and it looks to have had a nice steady climb since it did its split (2 shares to at $40). The long term prospects for the company looks favorable. If the market backs off and this stocks drops down to around $44 or $45 and seems to find a new bottom at this range, I would jump back in and buy some October or November calls, buying them far enough out and waiting for a market turn around. This is the kind of play that I will be looking for. There could be individual slams amidst a sector that is going up and there can also be a lot of losers. I will just get more selective now, and take on a little bear market strategy of looking for the diamonds in the hay stack. I will be more selective and a lot more careful. That's probably not bad advice for anytime in the market place, but more so right now. If the market does soften, the options that I have been buying may not materialize with profits as quickly as before.

Chiron (CHIR) is down 0.75 for the day. It is $98.50 x $99.25. I made a lot of money on this one when they made the announcement. I got in and got out. I still have some of the options that I bought when the stock was at $102. I made a lot of profits on this already—way more than enough to offset the few little losses that I am going to have. It is down again, and the 4:1 stock split is coming up in August. I put in an order to buy the August $95 calls which were $9 x $9.375. I put in an order to buy the August $100 calls which were $6.825 x $7. I am going to try to get the best price that I can. I told my stockbroker to keep an eye on these and get out of the August $95 calls at around $13-$14, and try to get out of the August $100 calls at around $10. I am reviewing some of my positions that are expiring in July. I have some options that were profitable at one time, but I held onto them for so long that they are down right now. I am waiting for them to bounce back up. Some *of them may not be able to recover by July. I am going to look at some charts today. I may buy some options further out. Even though I may lose some money on these short term options, I may jump back in and buy some longer term options, if the charts look good.*

I have a suspicion that the more these stocks run up one or two months before the stock splits, the higher the likelihood that they may not be able to sustain the run, unless they have a lot of good news coming out. I like stocks that are flat around the time of the stock split announcement. I always feel that I am not one of the insiders and there are all these people out there that know about a company announcing a stock split way before we know anything about it. This causes the stock to have a tremendous run up. It is just plain worrisome because it is hard for the stock to maintain that kind of momentum. When I hear about these new companies, I am going to be more diligent about checking the charts before I jump in just because the company is doing a stock split. I think that everyone else should do that also. We need to check the basic fundamentals of the company. I have been doing that on a lot of these companies, but sometimes I get caught up in the euphoria of the moment. I am just going to make sure that the underlying stock is a good play and that the stock is trading at a good multiple of earnings.

Enviropur (EPURQ) had a ticker symbol change. Now they have a "Q" on the end. It is now EPURQ. Usually when they add a "Q" on end, it is a company that is in bankruptcy. The stock has reflected such a move. It is $7/32 x $9/32. I hope it establishes a new roll down here.

Hewlett-Packard (HWP) was down just a little bit. The stock was around $92.375 x $92.625. I am going to do a "squeeze" play. These kind of plays are only good for the stout of heart. The

July $90 calls were $3.75. Approximately $2.50 of this option is intrinsic value. The other dollar plus is time value. Obviously, there is not much time left, but it is doing a 2:1 split on the 15th of July. I will hope for a bounce back. I also purchased the August $95 calls for backup insurance. They were $3.875 x $4.25. I purchased 10 contracts of each of these positions.

I am noticing in my trades that I have been doing a lot of slightly in-the-money options especially in the near term. I still think that this is a good and conservative play. I have got a lot of letters from people who are commenting that they are getting a bigger bang for their buck when they purchase slightly out-of-the-money options. In this case, they would buy the $75 strike price out a month or two or three. I agree. From my own historical experience, this is a very true statement. If the stock does move a lot, you are going to get a bigger bang for your buck. If you buy in-the-money options, you will be picking up a better Delta formula, i.e. there is a closer relationship between the stock and the option. If you are doing a short term play, I still like the in-the-money options. However, I am going to play quite a few options on these stocks that have hit their support level using this slightly out-of-the-money play.

Good morning everyone. Hewlett-Packard (HWP) has taken a $10 slam today. The last time I checked, it was at $79, so I checked on the August options. I was looking for a quick dead cat bounce-to get in and get out. Remember, this stock is also coming up on a 2:1 stock split. The August $75 calls were trading around $6.375 x $7.50, the August $80 calls were trading around $4 x $4.25, and the August $85 calls were trading around $2 x $2.375. I checked further out and there were no November $80 calls. The only November calls that were close to the stock price were the November $85 calls and they were trading around $5.50 x $5.875. I purchased ten contracts of the August $80 calls and ten contracts *of the November $85 calls. Both at the market. I want to ride the November calls through the split.*

I also went long on a stock to build up my portfolio. The company is Broderbund Software (BROD) and the stock was trading around $30.75 x $31.25, but it fell down $1 in about five minutes. I hope to buy it around $30.25 and I put my order in for 100 shares.

United Health Care (UNH) dropped from $44 in the last couple of days to $31. I was checking on the August options to see if I could do a dead cat bounce, but there are no $30 calls or $35 calls. The August $40 calls are 25¢. I checked way out in December and they have December $30 calls, but my broker could not get a price on them. The December $35 calls closed yesterday at $2.50 and the December $40 calls closed yesterday at $1.375. So, I placed my order for 20 contracts of the December $35 calls for $2.50. Then I thought, "what the hey, I could risk $250 and play the August $40 calls." It would only be $1 or $2 movement in the stock and that 25¢ option could easily go to 50¢. But, this is a very risky play, because it is $9 out of the money and it has only five weeks to get back up there.

There is a 3:1 stock split announcement on Paravant (PVAT). I placed an order to purchase 1,000 shares in one account and another 1,000 shares in a different account. This stock is trading around $15. It did its IPO a few months ago in the $5 range. This is unusual for a stock to do a split so soon after its IPO.

Good morning everyone. This has been a most unusual two days. With the market zigzagging like it was yesterday, it was not for the faint of heart at all. I will make a few comments on the market in general, and again, I am no sage on this sort of thing. A lot of the volatility is in the high-tech arena and it seems to me that there is nothing in these high-tech companies including IBM

(IBM), Microsoft (MSFT) and Hewlett-Packard (HWP), in the actual day-to-day operations or the profit making earnings that they are actually accomplishing, that would justify such wild swings in their stock. Just keep that in mind. The companies seem to be solid, they are expanding, growing and they have good earnings. To see their stock up and down like it has been, there is no justification for it except for just a fickle market place and a lot of investor sentiment. For example, if you read my comments yesterday, I was sad that I had a GTC order on buying Avon (AVP) July $40 calls at $2.25, and I should have just put in a day order only, because I forgot about this order. When the order was hit, within minutes they dropped to $1.50. I could have lost money, in that they are July calls which expire on Friday. I considered this money gone and chalked it up to a mistake that I played on a GTC order instead of a day order, or in that I did not cancel the GTC order. Anyway, I had my stockbroker put in an order to sell them at $2.50, which he did. With the volatility of the market, I was expecting to lose money, but I ended up making money.

With Synopsys (SMPS), I did this play in front of the Wall Street Workshop in Seattle. I was telling them about rolling stocks and rolling options and one of my old favorites has been Synopsys (SNPS). The stock has been quite high lately, but it came down to the $30 range. I bought the September $30 calls at $3.25 and I sold them yesterday for $5.25. I bought the September $35 calls at $1.866 and I sold them yesterday for $2.50. That was a nice two to three hour profit.

Two days ago, I purchased Microsoft (MSFT) August $115 calls for $4.25 and I sold them this morning for $6.25. Microsoft (MSF) is currently trading around $116.125. Several months ago, I purchased the October $120 calls for $8.50 and they have been up and down. Two days ago I purchased ten more contracts of the October $120 calls for $5.50 and just a few minutes ago I sold ten contracts at $7.375. If you take it from the $8.50 purchase price, it would be a loss, but on the $5.50 price I am up. I went ahead and placed my order to sell the other ten contracts (whichever the other ten contracts are, for accounting purposes I will have to have my CPA figure it out) at $9. I am trying to get out at a profit.

Checking on several other slams, there are quite a few of them out there including Xerox (XRX). Xerox (XRX) is trading around $47.125 and it has done a 3:1 stock split. It was trading around $51 or $52. The August $50 calls are trading around 13/16 which is a little bit tight, but the October $50 calls are trading around $1.437 x $1.145, so I placed my order for ten contracts on those. I told my broker as soon as that order hits, to place a sell order at $3.50.

I did the same with Coca Cola (KO). The stock has climbed up to the $50 range and it is down to the $46 range. The November $45 calls are trading around $3.875 x $4.125 and the November $50 calls were trading around $1.50 x $1.75. I checked on a shorter term play, the August $45 calls (which are in-the-money) and they are trading around $2.125 x $2.625. The stock is at $46.375 and I am buying the options for $2.625. I am only paying $1.375 for the actual time value and I have until August for the stock to get close to $50 or above. I bought ten contracts of each, the November $45 calls, the November $50 calls and the August $45 calls. I then told my stockbroker to place an order to sell the November $45 calls at $6.50, the November $50 calls at $3, and the August $45 calls at $3.625. I am learning another lesson here, that when I get so busy that I can't follow my plays, it is better to put in an order to sell them as soon as I buy them even though I may miss out of some potential profits. A lot of times, I have had my options run up in value and I did not get out of them and they go down to under where I purchased them and I could have had a 20%, 30%, or 40% profit in a matter of days.

United Airlines (UAL) was at $46 x $46.125. I bought 200 shares. I want you to think this one through with me and rationalize where the stock is. When the company announced a stock split several months ago, the stock was around $178. It ran up to $190, $200, $220, then back to $200, then up to $210, then back to $195, then up to $200. It was very volatile stock. It was around $220 when it did the 4:1 split. This would be $55. It went up and down after the split. It is currently around $46, which would put the stock at $184. This is about where it was before they announced the split. They just announced great earnings. It popped up and now it is down a little bit. This is why I bought 200 shares to build up my portfolio. I think there are a lot of option plays on this one also. I think that this is a good, solid company and I want to start building up shares.

I did do a play on Chiron (CHIR). Remember it is coming up on a 4:1 stock split this Friday and the exdividend date will be Monday. The stock closed Friday at $85.50. The September $80 calls were trading around $10.50, the September $85 calls were trading around $7.625 and the September $90 calls were trading around $5.375. I placed my order for ten contracts of each of those options. I then told my stockbroker to put in an order to sell the September $80 calls at $13.50, the September $85 calls at $10, and the September $90 calls at $7.50. With its stock split on Friday, there may be a $2 to $3 run up in the stock. I just want to play the options for a $2 or $3 profit and get out. I will wait until after the stock split to see if it backs off a little and then I may jump back in. I love these 4:1 stock splits, and I have also seen a tremendous run up in a stock right around its split date, and then back off at or below its pre-split prices.

We did a play on Gaylord Container (GCR) that we would like to pass on to you. We sold the puts and bought the calls. Please be sure to do your own homework and check with your own professionals before purchasing any stock. We sold the September $10 puts on Gaylord Container (GCR) at $2.75. Then, we bought the August $7.50 calls on Gaylord Container (GCR) at 25¢, and the September $7.50 calls at 62.5¢. We also purchased the December $7.50 calls at $1.052, the December $10 calls at 50¢, and the March $7.50 calls at $1.625. The money from the sale of the puts covered the purchase of the calls. We are in these options at little or no cost. If the stock does go up, we have not only made money, but we have paid for the trade before we ever made the money. Again, please be sure to do your own homework and check with your own professionals before purchasing any stock.

I read about TBC, Inc. (TBCC) in a magazine article. They mentioned in the article that they would recommend the stock up to a $10 purchase price. The stock was trading at $6.875 x $7.125. I put in an order to buy 1,000 shares. I am selling the September $7.50 calls for 75¢. Also, I did another play on this stock. You have to follow me through on this one to see that the cash flow part of this is a wash. I sold some puts and generated some cash flow. Also, I bought some calls. Remember, this is our tandem play— sell a put/buy a call. This is thinking that the stock is going to go back up to the $10-$11 range. If you have a chance to run a chart on this one, you will notice that it has been down in the $6 range, but it has also been up to $10-$11. The momentum is on a rise in the stock right now. I sold the December $10 puts for $3.25. I am agreeing to have someone sell me the stock at $10, but when I am picking up $3.25, it is the equivalent of buying the stock at $6.75. Remember, when you are selling puts, you need to like the company at a particular price. I am not thrilled about the stock at $10, but the cost basis of $6.75 would not be too bad. Obviously, this is before commissions are taken out. By selling the puts, I generated $3,250. Also, I bought the March $5 calls for $2.625. The stock is at $7.125, therefore $2.125 of this is in-the-money and I am only paying 37.5¢ for the time premium between now and March 1997. There should be almost a tick for tick with the stock. If the stock goes up $1, the March $5 calls should go to $3.50 or so. Obviously, none of this is guaranteed, but when it is so far in-the-money, it looks like a good deal. The reason I bought the $5 calls instead of the $7.50 calls is because there was only a small difference in the price, so by paying a little bit more money, I picked up the lower $5 strike price which is a $2.50 reduction in the cost of the stock. I also bought the December $7.50 calls at 87.5¢.

Cascade Communications (CSCC) is trading around $68. I sold the September $55 puts for $1.50. Now, these are way-out-of-the-money puts. This is a $68 stock and I am selling the $55 put, so it would have to take a $13 drop for it to get put to me. Usually, you sell puts when you think the stock is going to rise and this is my hope in this case too. Cascade Communications (CSCC) looks to be on a dip and if the stock goes back up, I could even buy back the puts and be free of the obligation. I have about four weeks before they expire and it would have to do a dramatic drop in the stock before I get these stocks put to me.

Again, these are very risky plays in that I am exposed and I would have to come up with a lot of money to cover my positions. But, remember once again when I sell puts, I am doing so on the thought that the stock is going to go up, that I like the company and I like the company at that particular price. By selling puts I generate income and it could also be an adjusted basis on the purchase price. I could adjust the purchase price by the premium I receive for selling the put.

Selling puts is fast becoming one of my temporary favorite plays. A lot of that has to do with the "July Thing"—a lot of stocks going down and now coming back up. Remember, when you sell puts, you are hoping that the stock goes up, so your puts can be bought back at a lower price, or have the stock go up above the strike price and not have the stock put to you. This becomes a cash flow generation machine with very little concern of having stocks put to you and tying up more of your money.

Right at the end of the close on Friday, I placed an order for the November $45 calls on US Robotics (USRX). I got them for $8.25. The stock is currently around $48.25 x $48.25 and it is up around $1 this morning. There is a lot of premium to pay for the option, $3 is in-the-money and most of the option money is out-of-the-money. This high premium signifies to me that it is a very volatile stock and the options market believes that it may come right back.

Hi everyone. I called a couple of my stockbrokers about Protein Design Labs (PDLI) to find out if the stock was at the low part of its range. It definitely was in the low range, but it was not in the lowest part of the range. This stock has bounced all around the last week or so between $14 and $17. It has been quite volatile. It looks like it may have settled down in the $15 price range. It was at $22 a while ago. I am not 100% certain that it has hit the bottom. It broke through its support level, and it could definitely go down back to $12 or $13 again. With the stock at $17, I was looking at it as a possible covered call play. That did not look so good to me. I looked at selling a put, but this didn't look good because it could easily go back down. When you have a volatile stock like this (it is not certain which way it is going to go,) it is really hard to do a play on it. I just kept looking at it. I decided to sell an uncovered call. I took a look at doing the September $15 calls or the September $17.50 calls. The September $17.50 calls were at 87.5¢, so I sold 20 contracts. I do not own the stock. In this kind of play, obviously, there is the risk of the stock going above $17.50. The stock would have to get up to $18-3/8 before I lose money on it. If the stock stays below $17.50, I just get to keep the money. In effect, it is free money with little down side risk from my calculations. Again, I have been wrong on this before, but not too often. You may want to check your own risk tolerance, see if you can do this kind of play in your account, and at least give it some consideration. Run the charts on this one, look at the volatility, and try to figure out for yourself which is your best play.

I just received a phone call regarding the Duramed Pharmaceuticals (DRMD). Our Wall Street Workshop is finding this as a good covered call play. I think this stock is in its mid-range. I sold the September $20 call at $1.25, because that looked like the best play to me. I went naked on this, i.e. I do not own the stock. This will be an interesting play and here I am doing these plays without looking at the charts, so I am relying on what my brokers and research staff are telling me. I really like to know the direction of the stock before I play it, because you need to know the direction and exactly why you are getting involved to do a naked put play and/or selling a call. You need to know so you can determine whether you should be buying calls or selling calls and buying puts or selling puts. On this one I sold the call.

Zenith Electronics (ZE) has a lot of good news coming out regarding the orders they will be receiving for their television with internet access. The stock went up $5 a couple of days ago, from around the $11 range up to the $16 range. It is currently backed off to $14.875. I am looking at buying calls and selling puts on this stock. I think it may weaken just a little more, so I am going to wait for a bounce back up then sell some puts and possibly buy some calls.

Good morning. This is Keven reporting on a trade that I placed yesterday. I reported that I placed an order to purchase the November $50 calls of Shiva (SHVA). My order did not get hit. The market started to move away from us, and my order was 12.5¢ too low. I am sorry this morning that I did that, because the stock has run up about $4 (as of 7:00 AM PDT). Sometimes, it does not pay to try and shave an 12.5¢ off the price of an option. If it is a good one and you want to be in it as it runs, it is better just to buy it at the market. For those of you who got in at the market yesterday, you are probably happier than I am this morning!

Paul also wrote a covered call on California Amplifier (CAMP). He had bought 500 shares at $7 a few weeks ago. The stock ran up to $10.50 and he sold the $10 calls for $1. This is a classic Wade Cook strategy, he bought the stock on weakness and sold the call on strength. If he gets called out, he will make an additional $3 on the capital gain.

We looked at SDP Communications (DSPC) and placed our order to buy the November $50 calls at $7.75. If you look at the SDP Communications (DSPC) chart, you will notice this stock did a stock split back in March of 1996 and it is now back in its range right before it split. A lot of times these stocks will get back into their pre-split range and start oscillating up and down. People may be expecting news of another stock split. If it comes, then it often runs up, if it doesn't happen for awhile it may just continue to oscillate. It is in that position now at the $52 range. The theory is if it does oscillate it should go back up to $55 or $56—we will see!

Micron Electronic (MUEI) was trading around $19. Remember, this is a spin-off from Micron Technologies (MU). It has had a tremendous run up from the $10 range that it was in a few months ago. I am looking at selling some naked calls on the thought that the stock may go back down. I will keep you posted. The market is not open yet and I don't know what they are going to go for, but I will be looking at the October $20 calls. I am not even sure that they are writing such a call, but I will let you know as soon as I do anything.

Another stock that I was doing as a rolling stock and rolling option was a company called 3Com Corporation (COMS). The stock is around $55-$56. If you look at the chart on this one, it seems like it is riding its high range. I may be looking at buying some puts on this one. I am not going to buy the puts and fight the trend of the whole market if the market continues to go up. I personally believe that it was nice to see the Dow Jones Industrial Average down just a little bit yesterday. It kind of mollified and pacified the bears out there. As we get toward triple witching at the end of this week, there is probably going to be a lot of activity, and upward pressure for a while with a lot of buying going on. As we head into October, I think that there will be a lot of selling pressure. Again, I never said that I was a prognosticator on where the market is heading. I just want to get good at individual plays. Again, I can not fight the trend, so if the whole market is going up in the next couple of days, I don't want to be buying puts.

I am definitely going to lose on my Microsoft (MSFT) September $130 puts. When the stock got up to $130, I did not think that it could sustain that price, so I did a short term squeeze play. I can try to get 5.2¢ out of them right now, so I am going to take the $60 and clear out. Once again, I have made a lot of money in the short term plays, but they also seem to be the only ones that I lose money on. I should probably do a back up longer term play.

One of the stocks that I want to report on is Iomega (IOMG). It looks like it has come back from the dead. The stock closed yesterday at $17.875. It is expected to open up around $19.

Whether it is going to sustain that level or not, I do not know. Remember, this used to be a very volatile stock. For the last month or so it has kind of been flat in the $14.50 to $15 range. I have a lot of shares and my average cost is just a little over $16. I had purchased some September $15 calls. Since the stock was under $15, they were kind of dead in the water the last few days. But now, the stock is $17.875 and I am going to get out of my $15 calls at a really nice profit. I even have some of the September $17.50 calls that were really dead. Now, they have been revived and I am going to get out of those at a nice profit. I have 3,000 shares of Iomega (IOMG) in one account, and I have several thousand shares in another. I have covered calls written on 2,000 shares. I sold 10 contracts of the September $15 calls and 10 contracts of the September $17.50 calls. If the stock stays above $17.50, I will get called out of these 2,000 shares at the end of day. I still have 1,000 shares in this one stock account that I may use to do a one day squeeze play. I may try to sell the September $20 calls. I want to see if I can get 50¢ out of these calls. If the stock goes above $20 today, I would get called out. If it stays below $20, I will just pick up the premium on 10 contracts. I spent so much time on Iomega (IOMG) this morning that I have not really spent time on any other plays. There are several other plays that I would like to try to do today. Keep posted because this could be a pretty wild day.

I purchased Intel (INTC) at $51 a while ago. I sold a (covered) call in August and didn't get called out. Then, I sold the September $85 calls and did get called out. I made a $34 per share profit on the stock and a $1.081 profit when I sold the call. I told my broker to WANGI (Watch And Get In) this one if it dips back down.

I am looking at playing some AT&T (T). It is way down. When I called a minute ago, it was down $4.875. It was down to $51.625 a few minutes ago and it is already back up to $52. The stock took a slam because of their earnings announcement. Basically, the stock lost about 10% of its value. It went from $56 down to $51. There are many Americans that own this stock in pension plans and funds, so virtually 10% of their portfolio value on this stock went down. I am counting on either a "dead cat bounce" or a selling put strategy. I want to own the stock and I can buy it now at wholesale. The October $50 calls were $2.625 x $3. The November $50 calls were $3.50, so for 50¢ more I can pick up another month. I placed an order to buy 10 contracts of the November $50 calls. I also placed an order to sell the November $55 puts which were trading around $3.375 x $3.75. If I pick up the stock at $55, I will actually be getting it for $51.25. This is a little bit under where the stock is right now. Again, this is a wholesale purchase of AT&T (T) if I do get the stock put to me. If the stock comes back up, I am hoping that the put prices will go back down, and I will be able to buy them back or just let them expire. I also put in an order to buy 20 contracts of the January $55 calls which were $1.50 x $1.625. Again, I was just hoping for a nice bounce in the stock.

Discreet Logic (DSLGF) is one of the premiere Canadian companies in software. The "F" on the end of the ticker symbol does mean that it is a foreign stock. The stock is way down and they are expected to make some nice announcements. I put in an order to sell the November $7.50 puts which were trading around $1.75 x $2. If I end up buying this stock, my cost basis will be $7.50 minus $1.75. The stock is currently trading around $5.875 x $6.125. If the stock goes up a little bit, I will be able to buy it at a discount.

I did go ahead and look at Safeway (SWY). The stock is trading around $41.875. I decided to wait for it to go back down, because it looks like it is in the high part of its range. I thought maybe I would buy some puts. I placed my order to buy the December $40 puts because they were trading around $1.312. The October $40 *puts were 31.2¢ x 50¢ and the November $40 puts were 75¢ x 87.5¢. So, for a little bit more money I was able to buy an extra month or two.*

I have what I consider might be a really hot play or at least a very active one. Lam Research (LRGX) has a very interesting chart. It is a good company that is nicely run. It has really good fundamentals and technical charts supporting the purchase of the stock. The stock got beat up a lot along with the other high tech stocks. It was around $25 and it is back up in the $28 range. There are rumors that it is a takeover candidate. Again, I stress that these are just rumors. I may have a nice run up—I do not know for sure, but I am going to play it. I checked on buying the calls and selling the puts. You will want to call your own broker to get your own quotes and prices, because they may have changed from the time I did this a few minutes ago. The stock was trading around $28. I looked at the October $25 calls which were trading around $3.50 x $3.875. I put in an order to buy 10 contracts of these. I also bought 10 contracts of the November $25 calls which were trading around $4.25 x $4.625. I also bought 10 contracts of the November $30 call options which were trading around 68.6¢ x $1.75. I bought 5 contracts of the March 1997 $25 calls which were trading around $6.125 x $6.625. I bought 10 contracts of the March 1997 $30 calls which were trading around $3.75 x $4.25. I am playing a lot of call options both short term and long term on this one. I also checked the October $30 puts thinking that the stock may go up. The October $30 puts were trading around $2.125 x $2.50. The November $30 puts were trading around $3.125 x $3.50. I sold 10 contracts of each of those. Again, I do not mind owning the stock. It is a nicely run company. I am looking at selling the puts to generate income and committing to buy the stock at $30 in October and in November. If I did get 1,000 shares put to me in October, I would be buying the stock at a cost basis of $27.875. If I did get 1,000 shares put to me in November, I would be buying the stock at a cost basis of $26.875. Again, I am generating income and I would be buying the stock wholesale. If the stock does go up and I do not get it put to me, I just get to keep the cash with no further obligations. I am buying calls and selling puts. I also went long on the stock for 1,000 shares. I told one of my stockbrokers, if I had enough money in another account, to buy another 1,000 shares on margin. I am going to buy 2,000 shares on, and I may be buying more.

Happy morning to you all. I think this is going to be another interesting day, like the past several days have been. The stock market is going up and down. The erratic style of all of the trading going on brings about a lot of opportunities. Iomega (IOMG) was weaving all around. ValuJet (VJET) came out with $600,000 capitalization. It makes you wonder if the hype and the hoopla can take it higher or if reality will set in and realize that this company is not making any money at this time. Once again, the stock market is not designed to make sense. It is designed to express the emotions and sentiments of a lot of people. Those sentiments are usually wrong, at least temporarily. As the reality sets in, the stock corrects itself. Our job is to try to stay ahead of that. When I say "our job," I mean you and me.

I am going to be loading up on Eurogas (EGAS). I am going to take a large position in this stock. I don't know how many shares I am going to buy. Then, I am going to try to get out of it around $10 or $12. The stock is currently trading around $3.50. I want to see if I can get a triple on this one. I think that there may be some good news coming out. I will watch it. Again, you need to do your own research. There are several market makers on this stock. It is very risky when you buy a stock involved in energy exploration.

I bought 2,000 shares of Janex International (JANX). I bought this yesterday right at the market close. I may buy a few thousand more shares this morning. I am hoping for a turnaround as a bottom fishing stock. Again, a highly risky stock. They were profitable a couple years ago and then lost money last year. I am hearing good things about it from a stockbroker. The stock was around $1.25 yesterday.

I also have 500 shares of Monsanto (MTC). I bought 100 shares before it did the 5:1 stock split. The stock is trading around $36. I put in an order to sell five contracts of the October $40 calls for 50¢. The October $40 calls were trading around 18.6¢ so I may not get hit on this order. I want to write a covered call, but I want to do it at the right price. If the stock does get to $40, it would be the equivalent of $200 on a pre-split stock price. Remember, this one was $150 and then it did a 5:1 stock split down to $30. It is already back up to $36.

APPENDIX 3

AVAILABLE RESOURCES

The following books, videos, and audiocassettes have been reviewed by the Wade Cook Seminars staff and are suggested as reading and resource material for continuing education to help with your real estate investments. Because new ideas and techniques come along and laws change, we're always updating our catalog.

To order a copy of our current catalog, write or call: The Lighthouse Publishing Group, 14675 Interurban Avenue South, Seattle, WA 98168. 1–800–872–7411.

STOCK MARKET

WALL STREET MONEY MACHINE
By Wade B. Cook

#3 on the New York Times business best-seller list, *Wall Street Money Machine* is best in wealth enhancement, asset protection, and tax reduction strategies you'll find anywhere.

Wade Cook describes many of his favorite strategies for generating cash flow: Rolling Stock, Proxy Investing, Covered Calls, and more. He also explains the principles behind using Nevada Corporations and other entities to shield your assets from taxes, and lawsuits. It's a great introduction to the Wade Cook formulas for creating wealth.

BLUEPRINTS FOR SUCCESS—*Coming Summer 1997*

Contributors: Wade Cook, David Elliott, Keven Hart, Debbie Losse, Joel Black, Dan Wagner and Dave Wagner

Blueprints for success is a compilation of chapters on building your business and making it function successfully; on education and information gathering; on deciding among all the different types of business you can become involved in; and a variety of other things necessary for becoming successful.

THE WALL STREET WORKSHOP VIDEO SERIES
by Wade B. Cook

Ten albums, eleven hours of intense instruction in rolling stock, options on stock split companies, writing covered calls and eight other tested strategies designed to help you earn 18% per *month* on your investments. Filmed live at a Wall Street Workshop, Wade Cook is at his dynamic best. By learning, reviewing and implementing the strategies taught here, you will gain the knowledge and the confidence to take control of your investments, and double their value every $2^1/_2$ to 4 months. Best of all, it will be all in cash, protecting you from any downturn in the market, and giving you an income you can live on. There is no other video in existence that can give you this information, or that can extend the possibility to you of becoming a millionaire in just three years.

Here's a list:

ALBUM 1	• Getting Started
ALBUM 2	• Writing Covered Calls
ALBUM 3	• Rolling Stock/Rolling Options
ALBUM 4	• Options/Proxy Investing
ALBUM 5	• Money Multipliers
ALBUM 6	• Early Bird Session
ALBUM 7	• Stock Market Dynamics
ALBUM 8	• Short Sales/Hedges
ALBUM 9	• Inosculation of Strategies
ALBUM 10	• Entity Structuring
BONUS BINDER	• Two workbooks to help you work through everything

THE NEXT STEP VIDEO SERIES

Designed for graduates of the Wall Street Workshop, this video series takes the formulas to the next level. Wade and his team of instructors go in depth into the inosculation of strategies taught in the Wall Street Workshop. They also describe the finer points of research, analysis, and fundamentals.

This advanced workshop will bring to life new and exciting strategies, variations on themes of other formulas, and revisit time honored techniques. New formulas for timing, entering and exiting plays, and new helpful hints to capture more profits are covered.

Volumes included are:

Volume 1   Quick Turn Profits

Volume 2   Profitable Charting

Volume 3   Rolling Stock/Rolling Options

Volume 4   Selling Puts

Volume 5   Writing Covered Calls

Volume 6   Profit Taking

Volume 7   Home Trading Tools

Volume 8   Shamu Combo

Volume 9   Technical Analysis vs. Fundamentals

Volume 10 Making it Work

ZERO TO ZILLIONS Audiocassette Set
by Wade B. Cook

A four album, 16 cassette, powerful, audio workshop on Wall Street – understanding it, playing it successfully, and retiring rich. Learn powerful investment strategies, eleven of them, as you drive. Learn to avoid pitfalls and losses. Learn to catch "day-trippers" and how to "bottom fish." Learn to write covered calls, and to double your money in one week on options on stock split companies. Wade "Meter Drop" Cook can teach you how he makes 300% per year in his accounts. You then will have the information to try to follow suit. Each album comes with a workbook, and the entire workshop includes a free, bonus video, called "Dynamic Dollars," 90 minutes of instruction in how all the strategies integrate, and giving actual examples of what kinds of returns are possible, so you can get in there and play the market successfully. A must for every savvy, would-be investor.

Here's a list:

ALBUM 1   • The Millionaire Mindset

ALBUM 2   • Writing Covered Calls

ALBUM 3   • Enhanced Returns/Minimized Taxes

ALBUM 4   • Exponential Returns

COMPUTER BULLETIN BOARD SERVICE

Wealth Information Network

This subscription computer bulletin board service provides you with the latest financial formulas and updated entity structuring strategies. The information is updated Monday through Friday, sometimes four or five times a day.

Wade Cook and his team Wall Street staff write for W.I.N., giving you updates on:
    ¨   What companies have announced earnings
    ¨   What companies have announced stock splits
    ¨   What options they are buying and selling

W.I.N. is also divided into categories according to specific strategies and contains archives of all of the trades so you can view our history. If you are just getting started in the stock market, it is a great way to follow people who are doubling their money every 2½ to 4 months. Log on, watch what they are doing, and learn from their example.

ENTITY INTEGRATION

BRILLIANT DEDUCTIONS
by Wade B. Cook

Do you want to make the most of the money you earn? Do you want to have solid tax havens and ways to reduce the taxes you pay? This manual is for you! Learn how to get rich in spite of the new tax laws. See new tax credits, year-end maneuvers, and methods for transferring and controlling your entities.

HIGH PERFORMANCE BUSINESS STRATEGIES
by Wade B. Cook

Your business cannot succeed without you. This course will help YOU become successful so your company can succeed. It is a combination of two previous courses, formerly entitled: "Turbo-Charge Your Business" and "High-Octane Business Strategies." For years, Wade Cook and his staff have listened to people's questions, and concerns. Knowing problems are solved by people who know the ropes, Wade's staff wanted to do something more. They categorized the questions and came up with about 60 major areas of concern. Wade then went into the studio and dealt head on with these questions. It's a comprehensive collection of knowledge to get you started quickly.

Here's a list:

Tape 1
- Corporate arrangements—getting the family involved.
- Using corporations to make sure your family gets everything.
- How to have multiple entities so everything is taxed at 15%.
- How to get complete liability protection.
- Using the corporation to control your assets.
- How the officers and directors avoid liability.
- How to have and use different classes of stock.

Tape 2
- S or C—which is best?
- Nevada reasoning
- Corporate pension planning
- Paper trails
- Making more—keeping more
- Needed licenses
- Bookkeeping techniques
- Part of the puzzle
- Bomb-proofing the business
- Reducing taxes

Tape 3
- You — "sine qua non" to success
- Options for the boss

253

- Your highest and best use
- Seeing the whole picture
- Special methods of achievement
- Priorities—not goals
- Leverage people
- Effective management
- Leadership—new ways and techniques
- Finding the proper fit

Tape 4
- Monitoring for sure results
- Bring order out of chaos
- Big results from a limited budget
- Closing strategies
- Enhance everything you do
- Presentations, etc.
- Innovative advertising ideas
- Getting more sales
- Workable ways to "Get Famous"
- Negotiate for more money

Tape 5
- Choosing business entities
- Tax aspects
- Determine control methods
- Analyzing structures
- Year ends and more
- Realize bigger profits
- Establishing workable solutions
- Fitting it together
- Faster asset accumulation
- Saving money

Tape 6
- Make it an "us" company
- Encourage failure
- You get what you inspect
- Choosing a "star"
- Innovation for the ranks
- Getting your "A" team
- Confirmation from the top
- Brainstorming ideas
- Support the troops
- Excel your growth
- See the whole picture

WEALTH 101/UNLIMITED WEALTH
by Wade B. Cook

Wealth 101/Unlimited Wealth "University of Money-Making Ideas" home study course helps you improve your money's personality. The heart and soul of this seminar is this: make more, pay fewer taxes, and keep more for your retirement and family.

Here's a list:

TAPE 1 • Enhance your asset base, leverage, cash flow, and income producing strategies.
• Bring quality to your investments.

TAPE 2 • Proper blends of cash flow, tax strategies and appreciation.
• Get your investments to work as hard as you do.

TAPE 3 • Active and passive ways to beef up your wealth potential.
• Using the benefits to grow faster.

TAPE 4 • Using the different forms and entities.
• Learn the real key to protecting your growth.

TAPE 5 • Insights into the "Three Entities."
• A full scale dedicated approach to controlling your financial destiny.

TAPE 6 • Learn the three reasons for proper planning: to provide for the continuity of your assets.

THE INCORPORATION HANDBOOK
by Wade B. Cook

Incorporation made easier! This handbook tells you who, why, and, most importantly, how to incorporate. Included are samples of the forms you will use when you do incorporate.

THE FINANCIAL FORTRESS HOME STUDY COURSE
by Wade B. Cook

This eight-part set is the last word in entity structuring. It goes far beyond mere financial planning or estate planning, and helps you structure your business and your affairs so that you can avoid the majority of taxes, retire rich, escape lawsuits, bequeath your assets to your heirs without government interference, and, in short—bombproof your entire estate. There are six audio cassette seminars on tape, an entity structuring video and a full documents kit. Look at the following sampling of what is in this set:

Part 1—CORPORATE STRUCTURING CLINIC

This first part teaches you to create a protective shield around your business and investments using a system of financial architecture for your personal and business assets that insulates you from loss and substantially reduces your taxes.

You'll learn how to break up your business into different legal entities and integrate them so if something should ever go wrong, a lawsuit, a judgement, etc. You're financially bomb-proofed.

Part 2—PENSION POWER

The word "empower" is overworked today, but in regard to your own great retirement that is exactly what this course will do for you—literally put the power in your own hands to control your financial destiny. You'll discover the ins and outs of money control. You'll see this "power-full" entity come alive. You'll be in the drivers' seat– a seat in a machine that will maneuver well in the fast track.

Here's a list:

TAPE 1 • Setting up a "safe harbor" for your money.
 • How to set up a self-trusteed pension plan.
 • How to immediately start saving on taxes.
 • Choosing the right plan for you.
 • How to avoid excessive fees charged by the big guys.

TAPE 2 • An explanation of the two major types of pension plans.
 • How to put aside up to $30,000 per year.
 • Determine which business organization to use.
 • How to combine the types of plans for maximum growth.

TAPE 3 • How to act like the big guys with your small business.
  • How to roll over money from existing plans.
  • Step-by-step process in setting up your plan.
  • Everything you wanted to know about vesting.

TAPE 4 • How to wear the different hats.
  • How to get the pension money to take on your personality.
  • What you can and cannot invest in.
  • How to aggressively get your money compounding at over 20% a year.

TAPE 5 • How to set up a "tax free entity."
  • How to go from Chevrolet to Rolls Royce in less than two years.
  • How to avoid capital gains taxes.
  • How to set up a plan to keep your money totally safe.
  • How to stay in control of your financial destiny.

TAPE 6 *(This is an interview by Wade Cook with one of America's foremost pension administrators.)*
  • Understanding the relationship with the plan sponsor, administrator, and trustee.
  • How to set up and operate a "self trusteed" pension plan.
  • How to make your money grow faster than you ever thought possible.
  • How to avoid all the common mistakes.
  • How to get really rich and get ready for a great retirement.

PART 3—THE LIVING LOVING TRUST

Living Trusts are a very important part of your financial puzzle. Every adult needs one, no matter how rich they are. For living, for death, they are an indispensable component of your overall financial situation. A Living Trust is far reaching and has a dynamism all its own. But it is not a stand-alone entity. This Living Trust Seminar explores and exposes all.

Here's a list:

TAPE 1 • How to chose the right vehicle to get to your financial destination.

- How to avoid probate, provide for the continuity of your assets and eliminate or reduce estate taxes.
- An explanation of three kinds of estates.
- The trust relationship explained.
- How to avoid the horrible problems of probate.
- An explanation of what a living trust does and does not do.
- The remarkable Q-TIP provision.
- How to make sure that everything is established in a tender, loving, caring way.

TAPE 2 •
- How to make sure all the proper players are in place.
- How to provide for your children and/or grandchildren.
- How to use the durable power of attorney.
- The pour-over will explained.
- How your living trust will control your other assets.
- How to keep it updated.

TAPE 3 •
- The problems with joint tenancy explained.
- How to use different forms of ownership.
- A complete explanation of the stepped up basis.
- How to become worth millions, but have your taxable estate near zero.

TAPE 4 •
- Complete explanation of the entities available.
- How to use an irrevocable life insurance trust.
- How to use Internal Revenue code 351 for transferring assets to corporation.
- A diagram of how to set up your family's business affairs.

TAPES 5 & 6 • These are the same tapes for review by friends and relatives - a synopsis of the extensive set.

The information on these first four cassettes is so popular that many people have asked for information to share with family members. We have included two bonus tapes with this course, entitled "A Living Trust Overview." These are about 45 minutes in length and are easy listening for those who need to have a good basic understanding of what the living trust is all about. A brief one-page outline is given in the back of the workbook. Our recommendation is to listen to this tape with whomever you wish would learn this information.

PART 4—FINANCIAL SAVVY

Each of these tape sets is necessary for understanding the different pieces of the puzzle. Financial Savvy is the "capstone" of Wade's career. It puts it all together. It shows you how to fit your own assets, entities, companies, family desires and needs into a workable plan that will be a joy while you're alive, and outlive you for decades.

Here's a list:

TAPE 1 • How to make yourself invisible.
 • How to split up your assets.
 • How a corporation fits into your financial picture.
 • Tax reasons for moving properties into a corporation.

TAPE 2 • How to use more than one entity for making money.
 • When to use an "S" corporation.
 • An explanation of the 80% exclusion rule.
 • How to deduct $17,000.00 every year for equipment.

TAPE 3 • 3 stages of wealth accumulation.
 • How to stay in control of your money.
 • How to avoid debt.
 • Rolling stock explained.
 • How to use zero coupon bonds.
 • Know your exit before you go in the entrance.
 • How to avoid costly entanglements.
 • The ultimate investment—your own gray matter.

TAPE 4 • Understanding what financial planning is all about.
 • How to chose a good financial planner.
 • Understanding money management.
 • The seven keys to wealth-building today.

TAPE 5 • The choices of business entities.
 • Why you should avoid being the sole proprietor.
 • Why a corporation is a great estate planning tool.
 • The power of Nevada Corporations.

TAPE 6 • How to fill out proper legal forms.
 • How to integrate the different entities.

- How to set up your partnership.
- How to use the "dispute resolution" agreement to avoid lawsuits.
- Understanding the documents available to you.

PART 5—AMAZING MONEY MULTIPLIER TECHNIQUES

Dozens of techniques for making more and keeping it.

PART 6—OFFSHORE TAX HAVENS

Highly advanced strategies for accumulating wealth and passing it along without huge tax bites. Includes a discussion of I.B.C.'s and the four-step method.

PART 7—TAX STRATEGY CLINIC

Two cassettes teaching you how to seriously reduce your taxes.

PART 8—ENTITY INTEGRATION VIDEO

Structure your affairs completely, and put all the entities together in a fully protective, wealth-enhancing system.

Real Estate

It is so important to keep your investments diversified, we also recommend these books, audio tapes, and video tapes on real estate investment.

Remember, Wade Cook, America's premier financial strategist, made his first millions by applying his meter drop technique to the business of buying and selling real estate.

REAL ESTATE MONEY MACHINE
by Wade B. Cook

This bestselling book reveals the secrets of Wade's system. As you will learn, you can make money regardless of the state of the economy. Cook's innovative concept for investing not only avoids high interest rates, but avoids banks altogether.

HOW TO PICK UP FORECLOSURES
by Wade B. Cook

Do you want to become an expert in real estate? This book will show you how to buy real estate at 60¢ on the dollar or less. You'll get there before the auction with no bank financing—the easy way to millions in real estate. The market for foreclosures is a tremendous place to learn and prosper.

OWNER FINANCING
by Wade B. Cook

A short pamphlet you can give to sellers who hesitate to sell you their property, using the owner financing method. Let this pamphlet convince them for you. Special report, *"Why Sellers Should Take Monthly Payments,"* is included.

REAL ESTATE FOR REAL PEOPLE
by Wade B. Cook

A comprehensive overview of real estate investing. Wade explains all of the strategies, and gives you twenty reasons why you should start investing in real estate today. Learn how to retire rich.

101 WAYS TO BUY REAL ESTATE WITHOUT CASH
by Wade B. Cook

Wade Cook has followed success with success: ***101 Ways to Buy Real Estate Without Cash*** fills the gap left by other authors who have given all the ingredients but not the whole recipe. This is the book for the investor who wants innovative and practical methods for buying real estate with little or no money down.

LEGAL FORMS
by Wade B. Cook

Numerous legal forms used in real estate transactions are included. These forms were selected by experienced investors, but are not intended to replace the advice of an attorney.

RECORD KEEPING SYSTEM
by Wade B. Cook

A complete record system for keeping all information on your properties organized. Keeps track of everything from insurance policies to equity growth. Know exactly where you stand with your investment properties and sleep better at night.

THE REAL ESTATE CASH FLOW SYSTEM
by Wade B. Cook

This six-volume audiocassette series, originally sold separately, contains everything you'll ever need to begin investing in real estate immediately, do so successfully, handle all of the business aspects and retire sooner than you ever thought possible. Just look at all the tremendous information that can be yours

Part 1: MONEY MACHINE ALL DAY SEMINAR VOL. I

Spend eight "jam-packed" hours of real estate education with one of the foremost experts in the country today. You'll experience a thorough, easy-to-understand seminar that can lead you to financial independence, wherever and whenever you're in the mood to listen.

Here's a list:

TAPE 1 • How to build up steady monthly income.
• How to get your assets producing more cash flow.
• Understanding the bottom line key to wealth creation.
• Ingredients for making the deals work.
• Choosing types of loans to assume.

TAPE 2 • How to get the good deals to come to you.
• Questionnaire for prospective buyers.
• The two key words for making a lot of money in real estate.
• Selling properties on a wrap.
• How to develop cash flow for 30 years.
• How to make money on every deal.

262

TAPE 3 • Understanding the three things that can destroy your financial empire.
 • Why and where you should incorporate.
 • How to set up your corporation to meet your family's needs.
 • Comprehending the 3-entity approach to investing.

TAPE 4 • How to use chaos to get rich.
 • Think big in bite-size pieces.
 • How to control without ownership.
 • Ownership-Control-Cash Flow: They don't have to be the same.
 • How to divide up your assets if you're rich or just starting.

TAPE 5 • Understanding the tax brackets.
 • Active and passive investments: how they don't work together.
 • How to lower your tax brackets.
 • How to protect existing properties.
 • "S" or "C"—which is best for you.
 • The complete explanation of the incredible asset freeze.

TAPE 6 • How to set up your own self-trusteed retirement account.
 • How to do the money machine in your pension trust.
 • Understanding the types of plans.
 • How to get your pension plan to take on your personality.
 • Learn the dynamics of the Family Limited Partnership.
 • Massachusetts Business Trusts explained and explored.
 • How to avoid probate and save huge amounts of taxes with the Living Trust.

Part 2: MONEY MACHINE TWO–NUPS VOL. II

Money—The Elusive Frontier. This taped home study course is a voyage of the cash flow enterprise. It explores new ways. It gives new insights. Wade Cook, the master cash flow strategist, will lead you in a full, all-day seminar, teaching you virtually everything you need to know to make quick retirement a reality.

Here's a list:

TAPE 1 • Why real estate is a popular form of investment.
  • Three benefits of ownership—how to get cash flow, tax write-offs, and growth all at the same time, and with little money.
  • How to avoid problems most small investors face—hassling with bankers, renter headaches, burying your cash.

TAPE 2 • Playing the numbers game.
  • How to make money on every deal.
  • How to find assumable loans.
  • Cash to asset to cash—the most powerful financial concept in America explained.
  • Secrets to getting cash back out of investments.
  • Finding properties at sub-wholesale prices.

TAPE 3 • How to get your offers accepted.
  • How to get people to take monthly payments for their equity.
  • Negotiating strategies for beginners.
  • The five components of negotiating good deals.
  • Closing costs—your key to getting offers accepted.

TAPE 4 • How to get real estate agents to work for you.
  • Getting agents to take notes instead of cash for their commissions.
  • How to enhance the value of the property.
  • How to use zero coupon bonds.

TAPE 5 • How to sell fast and at the right price.
  • How to save huge amounts of money on title insurance.
  • How to double your income in future years with no more work.
  • Supercharged ways to process multiple properties.
  • The only way to make the rental game work.
  • How to build an incredible asset base and spread out the tax consequences over 30 years—the installment sale update.
  • How to fill out IRS form 6252.

TAPE 6 • How to quit acting like an employee and start acting like a business owner.
• Helpful hints—business cards, mobile phones.
• Entities to use—family limited partnerships, corporations.
• The problems with joint tenancy.
• Introduction to living trust.

Part 3: START SMART REAL ESTATE INVESTING

This cassette tape package will lead you to all the "good deals" you will ever want. As you listen you will be able to go from finding these good deals to actually writing them. This package contains six cassette tapes plus a workbook manual.

Here's a list:

TAPE 1 • The secret of leveraging money—only real estate buys and pays for its self.
• How to avoid three problems that stop people from making a lot of money.
• Instructions on the steps leading up to the Money Machine.

TAPE 2 • The type of assumable loans to look for.
• How to assume low interest rate loans.
• The ABC offer method.
• How to structure each property to produce monthly income.

TAPE 3 • How to get more deals coming your way than you can handle.
• Properties have problems, people have problems—how to operate so everybody wins.
• Real estate agents can make you rich.
• Effective advertising techniques.
• Other "little known ways" to find super bargains.

TAPE 4 • How to determine value in a property.
• How to determine the marketability of a property.
• How to only find properties that can resell quickly.

- Make sure all terms and conditions of buying are conducive to selling.
- Low cost fix-up techniques to enhance the selling price.

TAPE 5 • How to bargain for a position of strength.
- Know what you want before you start negotiating.
- How to choose a good team of professionals.
- How to keep offers simple and powerful.
- How to make sure that the deal holds together.
- Effective use of the property analysis sheets to get the best terms possible.

TAPE 6 • An explanation of the key components of an offer.
- A full explanation of the term, "and/or assigns."
- How to fill out the forms as individuals, corporations, or partnerships.
- Using the legal documents to answer questions.
- Proper terminology and how to deal with the sellers' equity.
- How to get immediate possession (if possible).
- An escape clause to get you out of the deal if necessary.

Part 4: GET THE LOW DOWN ON REAL ESTATE

This all day seminar on the innovative and effective techniques that Wade Cook has collected and used for the last fifteen years to buy real estate with little or no cash. Now you won't have to let the good ones pass you by. Use these methods to build a strong asset-based cash flow portfolio.

Here's a list:

TAPE 1 • How to get three benefits of real estate ownership with one purchase.
- How low or nothing down deals let you increase wealth exponentially.
- How to make sure all of your investments are measurable.
- Avoiding the common mistakes.
- How to chose your own style of investing.
- How to find the right properties.

TAPE 2 • How to lower the tension when making offers.
   • How to find sellers who want to sell more than you want to buy.
   • How to use the multiple offer to tie up super bargain properties.
   • One sure way to find properties when no one else knows about them.

TAPE 3 • How to get total owner carry back.
   • Understanding assumable loans.
   • How to use the exculpatory clause.
   • Negative amortization = positive capital appreciation.
   • Phrases to make the deal work for you.
   • How to cut title insurance costs.

TAPE 4 • How to come up with kickers to sweeten the deal.
   • How to make ridiculous offers.
   • How to use other things rather than cash for down payments.
   • How to postpone making your payments.

TAPE 5 • How to raise money if you're dead broke.
   • How to get the seller cash—but not your cash.
   • Information on Title 1 FHA home improvement loans.
   • How to get the seller to get a new loan that you can assume.

TAPE 6 • Government programs that work.
   • How to shift collateral.
   • How to use bonds to buy real estate.
   • Effective techniques to get agents to take monthly payments rather than cash.

TAPE 7 • The money machine process as a nothing down technique.
   • How to get an "infinite" return on your money.
   • How to use each property as a springboard for the next property.
   • How to create more cash flow than you can spend.

TAPE 8 • How to use existing rents for your down payment.
   • How to assume liens to avoid putting in a lot of cash.
   • Understanding subordination.
   • How to get going and start making offers.

Part 5: PRE–FORECLOSURE SYSTEM—
GET IT BEFORE THE AUCTION

At last, a complete approach to foreclosures. This system gives you a personal seminar for a fraction of the seminar cost and the chance to repeat the course free of charge. You can take notes in the workbook and learn at your own pace. Because there is so much money to be made in foreclosures, Mr. Cook has put the processing forms in the back of this workbook. Section 2 is blank forms that you can copy and use for your own deals. Section 3 is forms that are filled in so you can see a property from start to finish.

Here's a list:

TAPE 1 • How to find properties before the bank takes them back.
• Alternatives to REOs.
• Determining if there are redemption rights.
• How to find properties way below market value.
• How to help the seller save his/her credit by making up their back payments.

TAPE 2 • How to find properties in early states of foreclosure process.
• A full explanation of the time line.
• Cure date, sale date, notice of default and notice of trustee sale explained in detail.
• How to save money when buying the property.

TAPE 3 • Where to find, and how to read foreclosure legal notices.
• The components of trustee sale notice that will help you process only the great deals.
• Using attorneys and real estate agents to get you to the deals before everyone else.
• Other efficient methods for finding these distress methods.

TAPE 4 • How to make sure the property is truly a bargain.
• How to get information out of the attorney (trustee).
• How to save money on the closing costs.
• How to make sure the existing loan is assumable and workable.
• Doing your homework—making sure you understand the proper chain of title.

TAPE 5 • How to find the homeowner.
- Make sure the proper people sign the documents.
- Make sure the deed is properly signed.
- How to get everything ready for quick processing.
- How to make sure, in finishing the process, that all of your i's are dotted and t's are crossed.
- The four steps to finish the process.

TAPE 6 • What to do with the property now that you own it.
- Deducting the expense of purchasing—things your CPA does not know.
- Make sure that by purchasing wholesale you're able to make a lot of money on each transaction.

Part 6: PAPER TIGERS

This is Wade Cook's exciting new tape set on the buying, selling and using of deep discounted mortgages. This seminar will get you up and going in this incredibly profitable business. This complete system will get you started from scratch. If long term, hassle free income is what you are looking for, look no further.

Here's a list:

TAPE 1 • The note buying business—why you should get involved in second mortgages.
- The four ways of making money in the note buying business.
- Explanations of straight carry backs and wraps.
- How to build up your monthly income in case something happens to your existing job or business.
- The four reasons why notes on houses are best.

TAPE 2 • The seven ways to find super discounted mortgages.
- How to effectively use the court house—hint, don't go after the new listings.
- Using real estate agents.
- How to get 40% plus yields on your money.
- How to compensate for wrong information.

TAPE 3 • How to do your homework quickly and efficiently.
- How to use the different questionnaires in the workbook to determine equity, yields, and offering prices.
- How to think through and make sure each purchase fits your financial situation.
- Know your exit on each deal.

TAPE 4 • How to find notes and make them better.
- Restructuring for unparalleled growth.
- How to double your money every seven weeks.
- How to increase the yields on existing deeds of trust.

TAPE 5 • How to attract investors to this business.
- Simple joint ventures made easy.
- How to use a small corporation to buy right.
- How to create a tax problem (we will solve the problem in other sessions).
- Ten reasons why people should invest their money in your notes.

TAPE 6 • Structuring your business.
- How to use the family corporation in conjunction with your other legal entities.
- The Pension Plan—a perfect vehicle for purchasing notes. *The appendix includes sample ads, letters, legal agreements and questionnaires.*

TRAVEL AGENT INFORMATION KIT

Have we got some exciting news for you! Because of Mr. Cook's extensive travel, he became a travel agent. Now, this is not like a full scale agent—he's an outside agent. Any reader of this book can be an outside travel agent with a full-service travel agency, but without all the hassles (computers, office space, employees). You'll save lots of money on hotels, car rentals, "FAM" (Familiarization) Packages, etc. If you are going on one big trip, or two smaller trips this year, it's worth it. This is not a travel club. You'll be a travel agent and the perks of being one will be available to you. Use for business or pleasure and if you choose you may also make a lot of money. Wade Cook Seminars has put together a Travel Information Kit. This kit includes cassette seminars, brochures, related information—everything you need to make a decision. (Price includes shipping and handling—$15.00.)

A WORD ABOUT COOK UNIVERSITY:

As you try to live the American Dream, in the life-style you want, we stand by ready to assist you. People enroll in COOK UNIVERSITY for a variety of reasons. Usually they are a little discontented with where they are—their job is not working, their business is not producing the kind of income they want, or they definitely see that they need more income to prepare for a better retirement.

The backbone of the one-year program is the Money Machine concept–as applied to your business, to stock investments, or to real estate. Although there are many, many other forms of investing in real estate, there are really only three that work: The Money Machine Concept, buying second mortgages, and lease options. And of these three, the Money Machine stands head and shoulders above the rest as a way of accumulating wealth very aggressively. The REAL ESTATE CASH FLOW BOOT CAMP is a three-day course designed to get your Money Machine well-launched. It is one of three major seminars within COOK UNIVERSITY. The second is the WEALTH ACADEMY a business enhancement through asset structuring, reducing taxes, and planning and preparing for the future seminar. The third seminar is our famous WALL STREET WORKSHOP.

It is difficult to explain COOK UNIVERSITY in only a few words. It is so unique, innovative and creative that it literally stands alone. The Wealth Academy has no equal. But, what would you expect from someone like WADE COOK? Something common and ordinary?

The quality and quantity of the information is virtually unheard of in this country. The WEALTH ACADEMY is setting new standards in financial education—leaving all others lagging far behind. The backbone of these concepts is the Money Machine—enhancing your asset base with assets that produce monthly income allowing you to live the life-styles you want to live.

We are embarking on an unprecedented voyage and want you to come along. If you choose to make this important decision in your life, you could also be invited to share your successes in a series of books called, ***Blueprints for Success*** *(more volumes to be written).* Yes, it takes commitment. Yes, it takes drive. Add to this the help you'll receive by our hand-trained experts and you will enhance your asset base and increase your bottom line.

271

We want to encourage a lot of people to get in the program right away. You could save thousands of dollars, if you don't delay. Call right away! Class sizes at WEALTH ACADEMY are limited so each student gets personal attention.

Perpetual monthly income is waiting. We'll tell you how to achieve it. We'll show you how to make it. We'll watch over you while you're making it happen. Thank you for your consideration. We hope to see you in the program right away.

COOK UNIVERSITY is designed to be an integral part of your educational life. May we encourage you to call and find out more about this life–changing program. The number is 1–800–872–7411. Ask for an enrollment director.

SPECIAL OFFER

Wade Cook Seminars has put these home study courses together in the most comprehensive format ever designed. Investing in the whole package could save you THOUSANDS OF DOLLARS!

CALL FOR DETAILS AND TO FIND OUT WHEN ONE OF THE SEMINARS WILL BE IN YOUR AREA.

1–800–872–7411

GLOSSARY

ASK - The current price for which a security may be bought (purchased).

AT-THE-CLOSE - The last price for which a stock security trades for, when the market closes trading for the day.

AT-THE-OPEN - The first price for which a stock security trades, when the market opens trading for the day.

BID - The current price at which the stock trades.

BUYING A HEDGE - The purchase of future options as a means of protecting against an increase or decrease in the price of a security in the future.

BUYING POWER - The dollar amount of securities that a client can purchase using only the special memorandum account balance and without depositing any additional equity.

CALL - An option contract giving the owner the right (but not the obligation) to buy 100 shares of stock at a strike price on or before the expiration date.

CALL PRICE - The price paid (usually a premium over the par value of the issue) for stocks or bonds redeemed prior to maturity of the issue.

CALL SPREAD - The result of an investor buying a call on a particular security and writing a call with a different expiration date, different exercise price, or both, on the same security.

CASH AMOUNT - An account in which a client is required to pay in full for securities purchased within a specific amount of time from the trade date.

COVER - 1) Future options purchased to offset a short position. 2) Being "long actuals" when shorting futures.

COVERED CALL WRITER - An investor who writes a call and owns some other asset that guarantees the ability to perform if the out is exercised.

HEDGE - A securities transaction that reduces the risk on an existing investment position.

IN-THE-MONEY - A call option is said to be in-the-money if the current market value of the underlying interest is above the exercise price of the option. A put option is said to be in-the-money if the current market value of the underlying interest is below the exercise price of the option.

INITIAL MARGIN REQUIREMENT - The amount of equity a customer must deposit when making a new purchase in a margin account.

INITIAL PUBLIC OFFERING (IPO) - A company's initial public offering, sometimes referred to as "going public," is the first sale of stock by the company to the public.

INTRINSIC VALUE - The amount, if any, by which an option is in-the-money.

LONG - 1) Referring to a person's position as the writer of an option. 2) Owning the security on which an option is written.

LONG STRADDLE - The act of buying a call and a put on a stock with the same strike price and expiration date.

LONG-TERM EQUITY APPRECIATION PARTICIPATION SECURITIES (LEAPS) - An option with an extended expiration date.

MARGIN - Effectively, a loan from the broker, allowing the investor to purchase securities of a greater value than the actual cash available in the account.

MARGIN ACCOUNT - An account in which a brokerage firm lends a client part of the purchase price of securities.

MARKET-MAKER - A dealer willing to accept the risk of holding securities in order to facilitate trading in a particular security or securities.

MARKET VALUE -The price at which an investor will buy or sell each share of common stock or each bond at a given time.

MARRIED PUT - When an investor buys a stock and on the same day buys a put on that stock and specifically identifies that position as a hedge.

MONTHLY INCOME PREFERRED SECURITIES (MIPS) - Preferred stocks that pay monthly dividends.

NEWS-DRIVEN - Referring to the volatility in the movement of a particular stock being affected by news, not by any intrinsic value to the company.

OPTION - The right to buy (or sell) a specified amount of a security (stocks, bonds, futures contracts, et cetera) at a specified price on or before a specific date (American style options).

OUT-OF-THE-MONEY - If the exercise price of a call is above the current market value of the underlying interest, or if the exercise price of a put is below the current market value of the underlying interest, the option is said to be out-of-the-money by that amount.

OVER-THE-COUNTER (OTC) - A security that is not listed or traded on a recognized exchange.

PRICE SPREAD - A spread involving the purchase and sale of two options on the same stock with the same expiration date but with different exercise prices.

PUT - An option contract that gives the owner the right to force the sale of a specified number of shares of stock at a specified price on or before a specific date.

PUT SPREAD - An investment in which an investor purchases one put on a particular stock and sells another put on the same stock but with a different expiration date, exercise price, or both.

RANGE RIDER - A stock that has a repeating pattern of highs and lows on its price range and gradually rises to a higher range over a period of time.

REVERSE RANGE RIDER - A stock that has a repeating pattern of highs and lows on its price range and gradually drops to a low range over a period of time.

REVERSE STOCK SPLIT - An increase in the stock's par value by reducing the number of shares outstanding.

ROLLING STOCK - A stock that fluctuates between its high and low price points for long periods of time and whose history makes it seem to be predictable.

SHORT - A condition resulting from selling an option and not owning the related securities.

SHORT HEDGE - A short securities or actuals position protected by a long call position.

SHORT STRADDLE - The position established by writing a call and a put on the same stock with the same strike price and expiration month.

SPREAD - Consisting of being a buyer and a seller of the same type of option with the options having a different expiration date, exercise price, or both.

STOCK SPLIT - A reduction in the par value of a stock caused by the issuance of additional stock, such as issuing two shorts for one.

STRADDLE - Either a long or a short position in a call and a put on the same security with the same expiration date and exercise price.

STRANGLE - A combination of a put and a call where both options are out-of-the-money. A strangle can be profitable only if the market is highly volatile and makes a major move in either direction.

STRIKE PRICE - The price at which the underlying security will be sold if the option buyer exercises his/her rights in the contract; the agreed-upon sale price.

TICKER SYMBOL - A trading symbol used by a company to identify itself on a stock exchange.

TIME VALUE - Whatever the premium of the option is in addition to its intrinsic value.

VOLATILE - When speaking of the stock market and of stocks or securities, this is when the market tends to vary often and wildly in prices.

INDEX